Unconditional

mental health redefined

Also by
MARA J JAMES

The Power of Piggie Bear®
Piggie Bear's® Power of Happiness

Unconditional
mental health redefined

MARA J JAMES

MJJ GLOBAL ENTERPRISES

Dana Point, California
United States

For my husband

AUTHOR'S NOTE

My amazing friend, the gifted healer Renata Ururahy, has helped me during the ten-plus years of my healing journey. Additionally, she has worked with me to create the exercises included within this book. I believe they will be meaningful for other families experiencing similar challenges. I am deeply grateful to Renata for her mindful contributions to both my work and life.

Each chapter in *Unconditional: Mental Health Redefined* concludes with exercises to help you on your own journeys of healing and discovery. Readers are invited to connect with me on my website, marajjames.com, for access to additional activities and recordings. Together we'll find the practices that support our nervous systems and encourage balance and understanding in our lives.

JOY grows from being present.

HEALING comes from feeling our inner truth.

TOGETHER we can redefine mental health.

CONTENTS
(see also: cargo, essence, insides)

INTRODUCTION

(see also: beginning, awakening, prelude)

*T*he first time she said it aloud, I knew she was right. "Mara, you had an NDE." My friend was referring to a "near death experience." Later, another friend looked into my eyes and said the same thing. "That was an NDE, Mara." Suddenly, I had a new way of thinking about what I had been through. And at once it made sense to me—it all clicked!

When we hear about near death experiences, we're curious. We rarely call the person traveling through this experience "crazy." But when one describes a dramatic spiritual awakening, something that changed for them as if overnight; something that might lead to ongoing examination, and ultimately a bipolar disorder diagnosis, for example, we react with concern or fear instead of fascination. We think that's an entirely different story. But is it, really?

I remember that day in my life as if it was yesterday, though in reality, it was ten years ago. It was May 2014, to be precise. I woke up in the middle of the night and began writing, not sure where the ideas were coming from. Then I began receiving "messages" from the television and radio. I was lucid enough to consider the very real possibility that I was losing my mind, but that didn't feel right exactly, because my mind had never been clearer. When I shared these feelings with my Rabbi, he said that "God speaks to us in different ways." I always say that if it wasn't for my Rabbi, my therapist, and the wisdom of my oldest child, I would have become convinced that I was batshit crazy.

Going through this spiritual awakening was only the beginning. I was determined to make sure that kind of "episode" never happened again. So, after being heavily medicated and finding my footing again, I began my healing journey. Who knew that this would have a profound impact not only on my life, but my entire family's lives, especially my middle child Jordan who had suffered his own challenges.

My awakening had shown me another side of mental health, a realm I had never considered before. Growing up with a mother who was diagnosed with bipolar disorder and a father who was a narcissist among other unsaid, undiagnosed things, I had a bad taste in my mouth whenever I heard the words "mental" and "health" together. I grew up in an era where "mental health" might even be said in a whisper by people who talked openly about physical health.

Having a child who was diagnosed with Asperger's and ADHD, and another with anxiety and depression … Did that change my feelings toward issues of mental health? Sure, but not so easily, and not at first. For a while, my children's diagnoses made me despise these words even more. It wasn't until I experienced my own mental health challenges that I was shown the gifts that accompany them.

I am grateful to have new understandings of mental health, to feel positivity and possibility to hear these two words together, to feel them connected at last to my spirituality. This is profound, and as a result I am on a mission to share this with the world!

Let's go back in time a bit. On the day of our son Jordan's first mental health assessment, I was a hot mess. The evaluator signaled my husband Kenny and me to step into his office while he asked little six-year-old Jordan to sit by himself in the waiting room. I almost lost it. *Who asks a six-year-old child to sit alone in a strange place, especially one who has massive anxiety issues?* This can only be a bad sign, I thought.

Typically, I like doctors. My husband and son are OB-GYN's and my brother is an emergency room physician. But to leave a child known to have high anxiety just waiting there, *no way*. But wait … Was Jordan truly feeling anxious or was I projecting my own considerable anxiety onto him? Wow, hindsight really is twenty-twenty. Still, it seemed so cold that our son was the subject of a series of tests to diagnose his behavior. I wanted people to know and validate him, not analyze him. I wanted acceptance and affirmation, not further confusion. At this point, I was already a warrior mom. I was grabbing for emotional armor to battle what felt like scrutiny.

After the evaluation, the doctor called us again into his office. These were some of the most unsettling minutes of my life. The doctor looked at his notes instead of our faces, held a blank expression, and showed little compassion. As Dr. Blank explained his diagnosis, all I could think was how badly I wanted to scream and punch him in the face. *This is an amazing little human you are talking about; this is our son, a brother, a grandson, my heart.* I began to quietly panic. Isn't a panic attack supposed to feel a lot like a heart attack? I stared at the little squares on the doctor's light blue tie to realign. This was the moment we received Jordan's official Asperger's and ADHD diagnoses.

Okay, deep breaths.

In the weeks that followed we learned about individualized services that would now be available to Jordan. Kenny and I developed a better idea of what we needed to do. Over time, we would see Jordan more meaningfully engaged in his tasks, better able to connect with others at home and at school. Our other children, William and Rachel, would discover how to support Jordan, the differences between helpful and unhelpful praise. We would become more mindful of one another as we navigated family life.

We had a child who saw the world differently. The things we knew about parenting no longer made sense. Our son needed us to be open to education, to be ready to ditch tradition, to embrace newness. Literally the definition of special needs, duh. Were we ready for this? We had to be.

We were referred to a new doctor, Dr. Day, who thankfully did look us in the eyes, and told us that family therapy will be an essential part of our weeks ahead. (Sometimes I called her *Dr. New Day.*) When moments of conflict or debate occurred at home, Dr. Day would ask "How did that make you feel?" None of us knew how to respond to this question, we were not the family that ever spoke about our emotions. Together and individually we had been managing these moments without processing or discussing our feelings.

Dr. Day redirected everyone in our household to an improved mindset. She kept up with William and Rachel's needs as well as Jordan's. The siblings of twice exceptional kids face their own unique paths, often on trails that become rocky and meander. It's a lot. Looking back, I am amazed by all three of my children, the day-to-day challenges they faced, their moments of collective strength, as well as the individual wisdom of their hearts.

Finally, we had the right diagnosis, a plan for school and activities, the best doctors and care practitioners, so smooth sailing from there, right? Not so much.

If I knew then what I know now, my life would have been much easier. I can't time travel of course, but I can try to pay it forward! In other words, I am here to help make your journey better. In sharing with you what I have learned and experienced through my family's challenges with mental health, I hope to help you decide what is best for you and your family. Together, we can laugh, we can cry, and we can make sure you have the tools you need as you make decisions for yourself and for the people you love.

In 2015, I was inspired to create a non-profit organization called Extraordinary Lives Foundation (ELF) to help children and their families experiencing mental health challenges. I felt that if we could work together and focus on the younger generation, we would have a profound impact on their mental health and emotional wellness and positively influence future generations.

I'm passionate about different types of healing modalities that can help a person heal and transform their own life. Admittedly, it was a process for me during my own journey to truly open my mind, to see the world differently, to appreciate the Universe in a new light. I want to help others to be able to experience their own healing and nurturing—without having manic episodes of their own.

Subsequently, I was inspired to create the *HUGS Healing Center* which provides a network of vetted holistic healers. These healers have allowed me to continue healing and enter into a new era of learning and transformation. If we want to move the dial on mental health challenges and help people suffer less, we must begin looking at complementary healing modalities, energy work, even past life regression therapies. I would not present these practices if I had not had truly positive experiences proving their transformational value.

It has been my honor to witness meaningful transformations for friends, family, and clients that could not have been achieved by medication and talk therapy alone. My own life changes required deep listening and radical acceptance. I was blessed in many ways by non-traditional healing as well as an emerging curiosity to learn more.

Coming from a family of Western-trained medical professionals, I never imagined I would be writing about holistic healing and encouraging my friends and family towards these modalities. My network includes experts in a variety of modalities including biofeedback, Body-Talk therapy, chiropractic healing, frequency therapy, hypnotherapy, Neuro Emotional Technique, Soul Memory Recovery, Reiki, sound energy healing, and the list continues to grow.

I urge you to try every modality that grabs your attention—it is a great gift to find something new that works for you. It is beyond rewarding to say goodbye to panic mode and hello to your spiritual strength, peace and happiness.

When I first started writing this book, I imagined I would create a parenting book. When a child has challenges, a family has challenges. When a child suffers, the parents suffer. Actually, the entire family suffers.

All around me people were asking, how did all of you survive that? Call me an idealist, the eternal optimist, whatever; I was never content to talk about surviving. I wanted to talk about thriving. I wanted to remember that before we can really teach our children anything at all, we have so much to learn ourselves.

I wanted to talk about more than how we survive that really hard day, even a manic one, or a magic one. I wanted to talk about how we find joy for all the days, whether we are children or parents or both. When I look around me, every adult I know is parenting in some way, whether they have one child, or ten, or no offspring at all. Because it's essential that we nurture and heal our own inner child as well.

This book looks at health and wellness not as an assignment, but as an art. With assignments we can feel restricted by rules, by other people's ideas of what a thing should be. We work towards a completed piece, waiting to be graded or judged. In making art, we are meant to be free, we are encouraged to trust our instincts, to make beauty from perceived mistakes, to consider that there are no mistakes, to arrive at an understanding that what we thought was a misstep or misfortune actually led us in valuable new directions. Works of art can be fluid and evolving, never really considered complete.

Just ask fashion designer Mondo Guerra, who is still sewing and perfecting his work as his model gets ready to step onto the runway. He continues to make alterations and adjustments long after Fashion Week has come and gone. Author Raymond Carver was known to mark up and revise his fiction long after a story had been published, always looking for new possibilities, recalling words and images that looked more demanding in the current moment than they had in the past. Art allows us to experiment, to grow, to continue, and to wonder. It lets us adjust our vantage point. It allows us to imagine something better and make that something a reality.

In chapters one and two we jump right into the hard stuff, the Art of Vulnerability and the Art of Sensitivity. In chapter three, we look at the Art of Stillness and its importance in positive mental health. In chapters four and five we discuss the Art of Intuition and the Art of Perspective. In chapter six, we do a deep dive into self-awareness with the Art of Reflection. In chapters seven through nine we explore the Art of Healing, the Art of Confidence, and the Art of Gratitude.

Among the aspects of this book I'm most excited about the exercises at the end of each chapter. With the expert assistance of my good friend and gifted healer, Renata Ururahy,

I have included exercises to support you along your life journey. My hope is that you will read this book in order, then return again and again to the chapters that are most meaningful to you in your personal healing journey.

I hope that you will make the exercises within this book part of your own ongoing daily or weekly mindfulness practice. The truth is we are all healing—we are all in training to become our best possible version of ourselves and need to find the exercises best suited for our growth. We are all in endurance training and becoming more dedicated. Honoring the self is an essential part of reaching any goal. This time we're in it for ourselves as well as for our loved ones and our community.

This time we are not winning only at the finish line; we are winning each step of the way, day by day, regardless if that day was a mountainous trek or smooth sailing.

So, onward. I say this with love.

Onward we march and grow.

1 THE ART OF VULNERABILITY

(see also: openness, amenability)

*L*ooking back to my kids' early childhoods, I can see that I carried so much anxiety and stress, especially with Jordan as he experienced challenges. I took each and every day as they came. I knew that I needed to do everything and anything possible to help our children live happy and successful lives. For Jordan specifically, I felt that if we didn't invest now in his future wellbeing, there would be a more limited path for him; he would not be able to experience the education and opportunities that his siblings and peers might enjoy.

I had married my college sweetheart at the age of twenty-six. Kenny and I were both New Yorkers; later we took the big step of moving our family to California. I have always loved the sunshine and warm weather. After visiting relatives from both sides of the family in California one summer, I kept thinking relocation would be good for us. I kept picturing our future days on the West Coast. Luckily, Kenny was thinking the same thing. Golden state, here we come. However, as the saying goes, you can take the girl out of New York but you cannot take the New York out of the girl.

I like to think that my mom, from heaven, had something to do with our move. After the summer trip to California, my father-in-law shared an email with us from a headhunter looking for doctors with Kenny's exact qualifications, hoping to fill some obstetrics/gynecology spots in Arizona and California. Five months from the day we read that email, we found ourselves settling into a new home and a new life. We were excited to raise our family in Orange County, California. Years later I would be especially grateful for our relocation as I was introduced to a community of holistic healers. There is no doubt in my mind that this is where we were meant to be.

But let me backup for a minute. When I was twenty-nine, still living in New York, we had our first child. I was amazed by the warmth and love around me when I became a mom. While I am not a fan of the word perfect, William seemed pretty perfect to me. He was a happy baby, easy-going, the kind of infant that makes you think you could do this ten times more. Okay, maybe not *ten*, but I held no hesitations about having more babies.

I still remember when I was sent to London for my work—a two-week business trip—when William was only four months old. As a nursing mother, I insisted that my company allow me to bring him. They agreed. They even provided me with a British nanny. The plane rides there and back were easy enough. I will never forget when we were in the black cab in London. I was just staring at this little baby sleeping in the car seat next to me. The cab driver, watching in the rearview mirror, saw my glazed over look. He asked me "first child?" I laughed. "Is it that obvious?"

Three years and four months later, we had our second son, Jordan. At first Jordan was an easy baby, just like William. Jordan had delicious round cheeks and the most beautiful big blue eyes that I have ever seen (which was bizarre for a mother with brown eyes and a father with green eyes). He was an amazing sleeper in those early days, and cheerful when he woke up from naps. He wasn't quite as chill as his brother had been, but that seemed true of second babies in general.

Then, two and a half years later, I delivered my baby girl, Rachel. Unlike her brothers, Rachel was born looking like a little doll with delicious *pulkeys*—that's what we called her super cute, chubby baby thighs. Suddenly my home was this wild place. My days were happily chaotic with three little ones at home. I remember how blessed I felt, also how tired I was.

As if overnight—I know people always use that expression, but really, in my memory, it was so sudden—our family atmosphere changed. I did not have the precise words to explain it, but I felt like the world was sucking the life out of our second son Jordan. I felt like the universe was saying to me, "Well, that was all fun for a while but here Mara, here is something new and scary to deal with, something you are totally unprepared for, so buckle up and good luck!"

My husband and I had grown up in similar Jewish homes where academic achievement was emphasized. Going to college was a requirement, not simply an option. In my husband's family, the unwritten rule was that they attend graduate school as well. So as our concern for Jordan grew, I kept thinking, *my God, he'll never go to college*. Perhaps that sounds strange to others, that of all the things I could be focused on, of the many things that required more immediate attention, college kept coming to mind. That was the potential future heartbreak that lingered in my brain—there were more, but that's the one I remember most.

I told my husband that instead of saving money for Jordan's college education, we needed to spend our money ensuring Jordan got the help and care he needed right now. He might never attend a university, but we needed to do everything in our power to make sure he became the best person he could be. We needed to find the best doctors, therapists (for Jordan and for our family), as well as parenting classes.

We knew this would sound crazy to our relatives. "Parenting classes," they would say, "oh please, you two know how to parent!" Some of our friends would be unsettled too. "What is there to learn? You take one day at a time." But Kenny and I were quickly accepting that parenting was a continuing education, especially now that we were parenting a child with challenging, unpredictable behaviors.

As Jordan entered Kindergarten, he was using his hands more than his words. His teachers noted his impulsivity and limited social skills. Before we could get a handle on the situation, Jordan was asked to leave his school. At that point we could not take it day-by-day anymore.

My husband and I had been the first of our friends to have children. I had very few people to confide in, no one who would truly get it when I described what was going on at home. I felt alone at sea with Jordan acting differently from his siblings and peers. My ego prevented me from opening up to new friends. I realize now that I did not have the support I needed. If I could do it over again, I would squash that ego and speak up. I would reach out for help.

Jordan became a very picky eater. He seemed to crave carbohydrates and sometimes that was all we could get him to eat. I am embarrassed to admit this but at a loss, I would feed him Reese's Peanut Butter cups. It seemed better than not eating and, in my mind, it was the only way for him to get a glimmer of protein.

In those days, I was always searching. Looking for the right foods, the right therapies; looking for answers. I cannot recall when the transition occurred, but over time Jordan became an amazing eater. As a young adult he loves *poke*—yes, raw fish—which he would *never* have eaten, not even looked at, when he was younger.

I remember Jordan in elementary school experiencing more anxiety and hyperactivity. I remember a time when we were at home, sitting at the kitchen table for lunch and

Jordan suddenly began screeching. I cannot recall what sparked the incident, only that it pierced my eardrums. Over time, these moments, his pain and my panic, had started to reverberate in my heart and soul.

I was not yet a spiritual person. I was not even sure I believed in God. But just in case, I was thanking God for ensuring I had met the right guy. There was no better partner for me on this journey than Kenny, I knew that for sure. He supported most choices I made to help Jordan and I had gratitude for whatever higher power might have allowed us to have these three beautiful kids. I didn't know what I was searching for exactly, but I was going to show God that he sent Jordan to the right mom. We were going to figure this out.

I was about to stumble on something essential and true. My goal for my children should be their happiness, not their success. There's an important difference. Searching isn't a thing we do in vain; searching leads to learning. In the words of our friend Debra Ann Afarian, founder of HBCC (Helping the Behaviorally Challenging Child), "God doesn't call the equipped. He equips the called."

Many years later, out of the blue, I experienced my first and only manic episode. At the age of forty-eight years old and not knowing that there was a Universe or a Higher Power, feeling skeptical as to whether God existed, I had a spiritual awakening. My family said that I sounded like a "crazy" person, and they weren't saying it lightly. They were concerned.

One morning, I was the only one home when I walked downstairs and heard a voice out loud say to me, "I saved your soul, now you will do what I say." If I wasn't in a manic state, vibrating at a high level, kind of how you feel after a few glasses of wine, I'm convinced that I would have dropped dead from a heart attack. I knew at that moment that my soul had been saved and that I had gone from darkness to light. I didn't know how it had happened, but suddenly I knew this in my heart.

When I shared this with my therapist, I was sure that he would lock me up. Instead, he looked at me straight in the eyes and asked me very sincerely if I thought that it was Divine Intervention. I asked him when he became so spiritual! The answer was yes, I did. This is precisely what I thought. And I knew at that moment that I was in the right place.

What was happening to me appeared crazy to others, but I did not feel crazy, and I realized that might be a precarious way to move through the world. Actually, my mind had never felt as clear as it did then.

One evening towards the end of my "manic month of May," which I now refer to as my magical month of May, I was in a store called GameStop. I saw three game packages called "Destiny" rise up into the air float toward me. I felt so light headed. To this day, I am still not sure if I said it out loud in the store or only in my head: *God, I know that this is my destiny, but this is all too much!* (He really overdoes it sometimes with the messaging!)

At that point, I knew I needed medication. The Universe was speaking to me way too loudly. Frankly, it was a bit too scary.

I ended up meeting with Jordan's psychiatrist. I already trusted her immensely. (Did you know that a Child Psychiatrist does the same training as an Adult Psychiatrist, plus two extra years focused on children?) Dr. D put me on three heavy medications. They made it feel as though the gravitational force had been multiplied by a thousand. The world was different and I was barely able to move. I was stuck in bed for weeks. I was grateful that they didn't lock me up, though I barely left my bed except to go to the bathroom.

The psychiatrist had asked me if I was having grandiose thoughts. I said absolutely! I was too embarrassed to tell her that I thought this God-thing was speaking to me. Growing up, I always felt that God was a big, judgmental man in the sky, pointing his finger at me, ready to scrutinize my every move. How could HE be speaking to me? I had been avoiding that guy for years.

No one ever taught me that God is inside of us; that we all have the ability to connect with him/her/it directly. God isn't way over there; God is right here, in our hearts.

The medication nullified my spirituality which is what I needed at that moment. But I couldn't help feeling sad that I wasn't connected like I had been. I felt grief and a longing for something that was no longer there. But what exactly was that something?

I swore that I would work hard to heal and be weaned off of all of my medication. What I needed was to connect with my newly found spirituality in a kinder, more loving way. I didn't know yet exactly how I would do this, but even in my weakened state, I was determined.

My family was still deeply concerned about me. No one was more worried than Jordan. He thought I went off the deep end when I kept talking about God. In his fifteen years on Earth, I had never done that. Suddenly, God was all I wanted to talk about. What if God was not a big scary proper noun? What if God was a verb? I was not fully able to ground myself or my thoughts—or as the kids say, dial it back. Even my older, wiser son was concerned when I wanted to wear flowy tops and spin round and round in the wind.

When I was told that I was displaying symptoms of bipolar disorder, I immediately thought to myself "Of course, two polarities, Heaven and Earth!

I will tell you this: knowing that a Higher Power existed helped me worry less and trust more. I learned that I was not in control of my destiny, or others' destinies, and this has taken a huge weight off my shoulders. I refer to the time before my spiritual awakening as BG = Before God and the time that followed as AG = After God.

There was a time AG when Jordan was in tenth grade and someone from his high school called me saying that Jordan made a "joke" in class about suicide. I asked where he was, and they said that he was driving home and that they sent a police officer to our house to meet him and us.

The old me went into total panic mode. I was shocked that they let him drive home. I started having visions of him driving off a cliff. I then reminded myself about my spirituality. I went into our backyard, took several deep belly breaths, and looked for a sign. I saw a beautiful Monarch butterfly fluttering right in front of me. I knew at that moment that my mom was sending me a message from Heaven: everything was going to be okay. I was walking back inside when I heard the doorbell ring. In walked Jordan, followed by a police officer. We all sat down and talked for a while. The blessing that came out of this experience was that Jordan agreed to see a cognitive behavioral therapist. *Deep breaths.*

When concerned for our children, spirituality has a way of escaping our brains. We go straight into panic mode. But we need our spirituality in those moments. Panic is fear but spirituality is peace, faith, love and trust and we all have the ability to be braver than we think, if we can just learn and remember how to access that part of ourselves.

Thanks to a dear friend of mine, a medical intuitive, I am able to sleep better at night because I have a better understanding of what is going on in Jordan's head. It took me a while to really own this level of faith, but after hearing it from a variety of healers, I knew that Jordan was not going to take his life. This was not the path he was on and it was important for me to work on releasing that fear.

If it wasn't for all of my intuitive healers, I would still be living with 100% fear and I *cannot* even imagine what my life and our lives would have ended up looking like. Thankfully, after a bump in the road, there is forward momentum ahead.

I am grateful to be living with a strong sense of peace, faith, love and trust. It took a beautiful yet rude spiritual awakening—and a lot and I mean *a lot* of healing—to be where I am today. I am forever grateful that my life has taken this turn for the better. There is way too much to fear in our lives. To be able to give this over to a Higher Power has been a true blessing for me. It is also one of the most challenging things to do!

After months and months of working with an amazing team of healers, in addition to my psychiatrist and therapist, I realized I had serious reserves of anger towards my father that needed to be released. Mara-the-Parent had been working hard for years. Mara-the-Daughter still had some healing to do. What did these two parts of Mara have in common? We were both searching for answers, looking for the path.

We were both accepting that the path could be treacherous and confusing. It could be smooth and reassuring. Most of the time, I did not know what was right around the corner. Was it supposed to be that way? Was I even taking the right direction? I was learning to trust my intuition. I was starting to see the signs the universe was lovingly sending to me.

I began thinking hard about the ways we learn from one another. We take learning for granted sometimes. Learning isn't as simple an endeavor as we think! We should learn about autism from autistic people; we should learn about Asperger's syndrome from people with Asperger's. Why wasn't this obvious to me, to some of the so-called experts? Shouldn't we be open-minded in all things? Curiosity is deeply undervalued in our current world. (Note: Autism and Asperger's syndrome used to be considered two different diagnoses. Today medical professionals consider Asperger's syndrome to be a part of autism spectrum disorder so they are in the same category of diagnosis. When I was getting started that was not the case. I tend to consider them separately.)

Let's not assume things are obvious. Let's remember to tell our children, our partners, our friends, that we are their biggest fans. Don't assume they know this already. Let them hear it with your words, from your voice. We are all vulnerable beings. And vulnerability is as complicated and difficult as it is exquisite. Vulnerability is soft, but still diamond-like in that it has facets, inclusions, color, and brilliance. Love your people; love them hard—beauty and resilience.

Actor Busy Phillips recently told CNN that she was diagnosed with ADHD at age 44, alongside her fifteen-year-old daughter who received the same diagnosis. Suddenly it made sense, she said. Even when she felt fine her brain was in "a spin cycle." She found it hard to prioritize tasks.

"The percentage of women that are newly diagnosed, especially with ADHD, has almost doubled in the last couple of years. We think we have to do it all or are we told that it's your job to do it all and hold it inside at the detriment of your own mental health and well-being," she said. Philipps added that with the right medication, a non-stimulant that works for her, she's been able to feel more organized. "There's just sort of more of an ease in being able to prioritize, being able to identify what needs attention and what can be put on hold. It's such a relief."

Where I live, in California's iconic Orange County, people love hiking. There is the Dana Point Headlands Trail known to be rocky and steep; the Whiting Ranch Wilderness Trail that meanders and is marked by red rocks, and the El Moro Canyon Trail that has challenging inclines but leads you to an amazing panoramic view of the Pacific Ocean. I think people love hiking because it's such an obvious metaphor for life's journey. But I'm also fond of David Duchovny's character, Jeremy, in *Sex in the City*, who tells Carrie Bradshaw he has finally figured something out about hiking. "It's really just walking." Sometimes we plan for magnificent journeys; many days we simply have to put one foot in front of the other.

I have learned that the key to living a truly happy life is to be vulnerable enough to realize that we all have layers of "stuff" from our childhood that can be released and healed. Many of us were told stories of how we "should" act and many of us were raised by parents that had their own set of issues. Some people think that it's weak to be vulnerable, but it is actually one of the strongest things you can do to improve your life and the lives of your friends and family around you.

THE VULNERABILITY EXERCISES

Vulnerability is an act of courage. When we hide our pain, we also suppress our light, keeping ourselves from true freedom. But when we bring awareness to our most tender, hidden parts and meet them with compassion, we unlock their wisdom and reintegrate them into our lives.

The following process gently guides you to look beneath your triggers and uncover the deeper wounds they are protecting. Instead of seeing emotional reactions as problems, you'll learn to recognize them as messengers—pointing you toward parts of yourself that need care and healing. With awareness and kindness, you can begin to release old patterns and create space for greater peace and connection.

Journal Activity: Embrace your vulnerability.

This exercise is designed to guide you through a process of self-discovery. You can choose to do it in written form, taking your time to reflect on the questions, or use our guided meditation to support you as you uncover deeper vulnerabilities.

Step One. Reflect on a triggering moment.

Pause for a moment and reflect on a time when your child's behavior triggered a strong emotional response in you.

For example: Mara recalls a time when Jordan had an intense outburst that felt overwhelming and frustrating. She felt out of control at that moment.

Write about your experience as clearly as you can remember it.

Step Two. Identify your emotions and behaviors.

Spend a few minutes reflecting on this challenging situation. What emotions surfaced for you? What was your response to this situation? What did you do in that moment?

In Mara's example, when she experienced Jordan's outburst, she felt angry, embarrassed, and ashamed. She couldn't understand why her son was acting that way, and in her frustration, she tried to calm him down by yelling, not giving him the space to process his emotions. This, of course, only made things worse.

Write down the emotions that surfaced for you and describe how you acted in your experience.

Step Three. Evaluate your actions.

Take a moment to reflect: Did your response bring you closer to the outcome you truly wanted, or did it push you further away from it?

When we respond from a place of connection and centeredness, our actions naturally foster peace, understanding, and resolution. However, when we react from a triggered state, we often create the very outcomes we're trying to avoid—more conflict, disconnection, or tension.

This awareness isn't about self-judgment—it's a chance to recognize when a deeper wound is driving your reaction. By using that moment for healing, you can begin to shift old patterns. As these wounds heal, your responses naturally become more aligned with peace, connection, and love.

For example, in Mara's situation, she yelled at her son in frustration. Looking back, she realizes that her reaction didn't bring her the calm or connection she truly desired. Instead, it led to more tension and hurt.

Now, write down your actions and reflect on the outcomes they created.

Step Four. Connect with the part of you that was triggered.

Now, turn inward and reconnect with the part of you that experienced those intense emotions. This part of you isn't your enemy—it's trying to protect you from a deeper pain, even if the reaction was overwhelming or unhelpful at the time.

Often, our strongest emotional reactions stem from old wounds—experiences where we once felt powerless, unseen, or unsafe. When triggered, our nervous system goes into protection mode, reacting as if the past is happening now. By bringing awareness to those deeper wounds, we create an opportunity for healing.

With kindness and curiosity, ask this part of yourself:

- What is the deeper pain underlying these triggered emotions?
- What is the unmet need that you are trying to protect or hide?

In Mara's example, when she thinks back to her younger self experiencing her son's outburst, underneath her anger, she felt confused and wanted the outburst to stop! That awareness was a breakthrough for her. It reminded her of her childhood trauma where she felt scared and confused as to why her abuse was happening and she wanted it to stop. In both situations, Mara felt powerless. Her unmet need was to feel safe.

Take a moment to journal about the deeper wound or unmet needs that may be at the root of your reaction.

Step Five. Embrace your unmet needs.

Now that you have connected with the deeper wound being triggered from this situation and gained clarity on your unmet needs, take a moment to visualize giving the wounded part of yourself exactly what it longs for.

Whether it seeks acknowledgment, comfort, or reassurance, imagine yourself providing it with love, understanding, and support. Envision this part of yourself feeling seen, heard, and completely embraced, knowing it is safe and cherished.

Take a moment to honor yourself for showing up with courage and compassion. This work isn't always easy, but each step you take toward understanding your triggers brings you closer to healing and growth. Remember, this is not about perfection—it's about learning to respond with love and connection, creating space for deeper peace and self-acceptance.

Additional Activity: Uncover your vulnerabilities.

You may also find it helpful to listen to this guided meditation, "Uncovering Vulnerabilities Behind Triggering Emotions," available at marajjames.com.

Start by finding a comfortable sitting posture. You can use a chair or pillows, whatever feels best for you. Close your eyes gently and bring your attention to your breath.

Notice the natural rhythm of your breathing, the rise and fall with each inhale and exhale. Let your awareness of your breath help you connect to your body. Now bring to mind a time when your child's behavior triggered strong emotions in you.

Visualize that moment as if it is happening right now. Let the memory come alive in your mind. Try to recall as many details as possible—where were you? What did the space around you look like? What sounds were present in the air? Was the temperature hot, cold—what was the lighting, the atmosphere? Are there any other people or specific sensations you remember?

As you take in all the details, notice the emotions that come up for you in that moment. Let yourself feel the depth of these emotions without judgment. Remember, it is okay to feel however you feel.

Now, imagine stepping back from the experience, as if you are watching yourself go through it. See yourself with compassion for the part of you that felt triggered. This part of you is not your enemy. It is simply trying to protect you in the only way it knows how. Even if the response feels overwhelming.

Often, the strongest emotions arise from old wounds; moments when you once felt powerless, unseen or unsafe. When triggered, your nervous system moves into protection reacting as if the past is unfolding in the present. But now, with gentle awareness, you can recognize these patterns with compassion. With each breath, you create space for healing, inviting a sense of safety, presence and deep transformation.

Now silently thank that part of you, saying "Thank you for your efforts in trying to protect me. I see that you were trying to help me feel safe. Are you willing to show me the pain or unmet need that you were trying to protect or hide?"

If the answer is "no," and this part of you isn't ready to reveal what it was guarding, simply thank it for its protection. You can try again later when trust has been built. Be patient with this part of you.

If the answer is "yes," and this part is willing to show you more, thank it once again. Then gently turn your attention inward to explore what's underneath your triggered emotions. What is the deeper pain or unmet need underlying those emotions? Take your time with this. Allow yourself to stay with the pain, even if it's subtle or difficult to name. There may be tender core feelings, or perhaps an old memory or wound emerges. It is okay if it's just a faint sense of a deeper pain or discomfort.

Honor the sensitive part of you. Acknowledge how much it needs your love and understanding. See it with great compassion, as if you were offering it the care and acceptance it has longed for. Ask that vulnerable part of you, "How do you feel?" Then ask "What do you need?"

Allow yourself to truly hear the response. This part of you may simply want to be acknowledged or might need a gesture of comfort, like a warm embrace. In your mind's eye, offer whatever support feels most nurturing in this moment, trusting that your presence alone is deeply healing. Bring this vulnerable part of you back into your heart with love and acceptance, embracing and reclaiming it fully as part of you.

Take a few deeper breaths now, feeling the support of your breath as it moves through you. Gradually bring your awareness back to the space around you. Notice how your body feels in this moment, and when you're ready, open your eyes.

Take some time to journal about your experience. What emotions or insights arose for you? What did you uncover about the deeper vulnerability behind your triggered feelings?

2

THE ART OF SENSITIVITY

(see also: awareness, sensation, receptiveness)

*I*magine having a professional say to you that your toddler has anxiety, or that your child has ADHD and is on the spectrum. When this happened to me, I felt like my husband and I were just given life sentences. My arms went limp as if my body was being literally crushed by the words.

Now imagine if that same professional would have said, *Your child is an empath. Your son or daughter has a sensitive soul. They can actually feel other people's emotions.* Imagine if the psychiatrist took the time to explain that this is a lot for any child to manage, but together, we will find a solution. Even better, what would happen if they said, *Congratulations, your child is gifted! And with every gift comes a challenge, so we will attend to those challenges and help to bring out the gifts?*

This would have been transformational for me. My outlook for Jordan's future would have been so much better. To truly understand mental health, we need to expand the focus of Western medicine. We need to account for individual energies, karma, and generational experiences. In some cases, we need trauma-informed care. It has never been more important to widen our vantage point.

Were you familiar with the term *empath* before you picked up this book? It's a new concept for so many of us, but there are empaths all around us. If you search *empath* on Google™, most definitions you see include something like "showing an ability to understand and share the feelings of another." But it's deeper than that. Empaths are highly sensitive individuals who literally feel and *absorb the emotional and physical energy of other people.* This can be a gift, or a curse, if one does not learn how to manage it.

An empath's energy and emotions become aligned with the human energy around them. I cannot explain exactly how it works, but I know that it exists. Similar to when I turn on a switch and voila! A light turns on. I don't know the logistics behind it, but I see the light turn on and know that it occurs.

Again, many of our children are natural empaths. The upside of this condition is that you have a child truly in tune with the world. The downside is that empaths of any age can become exhausted, anxious, depressed, and burned out from sensory and emotional overload. And little ones often feel these BIG emotions that they do not yet know how to handle. The complexity of other people's emotions can be simply too much.

Once I learned about empaths, I had an *ah-ha* moment! When I was younger, I always had a hard time going into a shopping mall, which made no sense; shopping always sounded like fun at least, and I liked seeing new things. Typically, I liked browsing around in smaller places. As I grew older, I started to wonder if I had ADHD. Much later in life, I realized that I was feeling all of the energy of those around me. A shopping mall simply had too many people experiencing too many emotions, whether relaxation and joy or impatience or frustration. Well, of course I was overwhelmed—that was simply too much to take on in exchange for a slice of pizza or a new pair of sneakers. It was confusing and exhausting.

Once I learned how to energetically protect myself (I will share this with you in an exercise section), I was able to walk through a mall and feel peaceful. I'm not sure that my hubby was entirely happy about this because it resulted in a lot more shopping for me, ha ha, but the change was exquisite.

Another transformational moment for me occurred when I was riding in the car with my husband. We were running late (something that often happened in our busy lives and it drove him crazy)! Kenny was annoyed and started becoming anxious. That immediately disrupted my happy- go-lucky mood. Once he saw that I had become cranky, he asked me why I was in a bad mood. I quickly responded "Because of the way you are acting!" Wasn't it obvious? Maybe not. I didn't realize it then, but I was literally taking on his negative energy and emotions.

I am grateful that I have learned how to create an energetic mirror to reflect back his (or anyone else's) negative energy so I can remain happy and peaceful while they stir in their negative emotions. It was an amazing trick that changed my life. In my mind's eye, I would simply hold my hand up as a mirror displaying his emotions for him. As a result, I would be reflecting the negativity away, allowing myself not to feel his "stuff."

Mind you, I didn't create this energy protection wall blatantly, in a way that seemed confrontational, which would have triggered more negativity. That was the last thing we needed. Once I learned this trick, I was able to happily and peacefully enjoy our car rides without having to feel his shit. It has taken me years (and years and years) to learn this simple lesson, how we cannot change other people, but we can change how we respond to them, and that's the key. Anyway, I wasn't going to let his *mishegoss* rain on my parade. If you are reading this, I love you honey!

"It is in our highest interest to listen to discomfort," Brianna Wiest says. "It's attempting to lead us to peace." After working as a journalist for *Forbes* and *Teen Vogue*, Brianna started sharing publicly her personal observations from years of self-inquiry and meditation practices. She has written several books about empowerment and self-reflection, and is a founding partner of *Thought Catalog*. Brianna believes sometimes the greatest gift life can hand to you is discomfort, because it allows us to understand what isn't working so that we keep reaching toward what will.

"Discomfort is not trying to punish you," she says. "It's usually trying to show you where you are capable of more, deserving of better, able to change, and meant for greater than what you're experiencing at the moment." Brianna reminds us that mental strength is a practice. "Discomfort informs you that there is another experience to have." Perhaps it's even pushing you to get out there and have it.

Empaths by definition are in a vulnerable position. They are open to all of the influences and energies around them. Adult empaths need to work diligently to set boundaries, to claim the space that allows them to protect themselves. Parents of child empaths need to guide them toward these same protections and for the young ones, we can do it for them. Often the work of parents is in providing context to a little human learning our big, amazing world.

If you are an empath, remain sensitive to your own needs. Keep your boundaries firm. No one intuits the world exactly the way you do. That is both your burden and your superpower. If someone you love is an empath, respect their boundaries and stay sensitive to their needs for solitude or rejuvenation. Be the valuable support system that helps your loved one thrive.

I remember when my children were young, taking them to a frozen yogurt store. They had their favorites. William liked strawberry, Jordan rocket pop, and Rachel's flavor of the day changed constantly. There were several families in front of us. A mom at the window in front of us was fumbling for her wallet, suddenly lost at the bottom of her everything bag— we've all been there—while her little guy's ice cream scoop with sprinkles fell off the cone and landed onto the pavement. A little girl behind them, who was with a different family and did not previously know the little guy with the ruined ice cream, immediately burst out crying. The injustice of it, of this boy being so happy to receive the afternoon treat of his dreams, then seeing it fall away from him in a split second—it was just too much for her to accept. I agreed with her. We both felt his anguish.

When you realize that you are or your child is an empath, there is so much that suddenly makes sense. Learning how to energetically protect ourselves and our children can be a game changer! Next time your child is acting out, take a look at what is going on around them. Are they taking on energy or emotions from their environment or someone around them? One of our healers worked with the parent of a high school teenager who had extreme anxiety taking exams in the classroom. The healer suggested that he try taking an exam in a room by himself, and as if by magic, he did not feel anxious. Before, he was energetically picking up on others' anxiety and a simple adjustment was life changing for him and his concerned parents.

How is your child, at this moment, being affected by the world around them? How are the people around them acting, including you and your family? Is your empathic child feeling and reacting to your emotions and your internal state of being, which might not be physically present, but felt on a deeper cellular, energetic level? I wish I had known about this when Jordan was younger.

Recently I was speaking with a client whose twelve-year-old son was diagnosed on the spectrum and with ADHD. We were on a zoom call when she started becoming anxious when telling me a story. I saw her shoulders begin to tense up and she began taking shallow breaths. At that exact moment, she received a phone call from her son's school and they told her that her son's eye was twitching and his stomach was hurting him. They asked that she pick him up from school immediately. I was grateful that she didn't mute me during our zoom because I was able to witness this amazing connection between her emotions and her son's emotional well-being. Once I pointed it out to her, she was blown away; I was too.

One day I had a meeting with a lovely woman, Sally, whose beautiful, angelic six-year-old daughter was diagnosed with social anxiety. The doctor wanted to put her on medication. This precious little angel wouldn't allow her parents to hug her and it broke their hearts. If you've been in this position as a parent, I don't have to tell you how disorienting and painful this can be.

I had Sally speak to one of our HUGS healers, who told her that her daughter was an empath and that it was too overwhelming for her to feel their big emotions, even though they were positive. Sally's daughter could actually feel the intensity of her parents' emotions when they hugged her. It was too much for her little body to handle. Sally and her husband had been heartbroken when they couldn't understand why their daughter wouldn't allow them to hug her. When they understood more about their daughter's gifts, they learned how to work with her, to take their time and not to be insulted, knowing that their daughter loved them immensely. That day, their lives had been transformed.

The immense love that Sally and her husband had for their child was so strong and was a beautiful thing. It was also overwhelming. And just as a child's digestive system needs to process smaller quantities and softer foods, this little girl's emotional system needed smaller, gentler quantities of feelings. Our connections to the people we love are powerful, sometimes more than we can even imagine.

Empaths tune into other's feelings, inadvertently and often with precision. As I describe this to you, your mind's eye is probably seeing one of your friends who is an empath or possesses strong empathic traits without even knowing it. In this way, they make wonderful friends, they are valued supporters and role models.

It's likely they were emotionally tired as children due to all they were processing. And they were forced into hyper-vigilance as parents. Just imagine that every time we feel anxious, fearful, sad, or angry, that our child feels our emotions too. Wow! Children will act out because of it.

With all of this in mind, we see how important it is for parents to manage their own emotions in order to help improve their children's. Mood regulation is imperative. Some children are so sensitive that they pick up on our emotions just by being in the same house, even when they are in a different room. And as I shared with you previously, my client's son was so energetically connected to her that he felt her emotions even though she was at home and he was in school!

I joke around but I mean it when I say that my poor children were screwed before they were born. I was raised by a neurotic New York Jewish mother then became one myself. (No wonder all of my children experience some level of anxiety and ADHD!) So, what can we do to improve this energy we inadvertently share?

We must learn to put our oxygen masks on first. Be courageous and take a long, deep look into the mirror. What do you see? Are there emotions that your children are experiencing that reflect your inner feelings? Please refer to the exercises at the end of this chapter to help guide you along this process.

Dr. Jody Carrington, author of *Feeling Seen: Reconnecting in a Disconnected World*, suggested something brilliant that lingers in my mind. She wrote, "Every time you think of calling a child 'attention-seeking,' consider changing it to 'connection-seeking' and see how your perspective changes." Don't be quick to say your child is acting out. Maybe, just maybe, they are reaching out.

Children are here to transform the world, beginning with their parents. They reflect things that their parents need to, or should I say, get to heal. If we take this to heart, as parents, we can work on our own emotional landscape and energy levels to ensure that we are being the best parents possible for our children.

In much of this book I talk about my children when they were younger and in school, but I need to flash forward to the present day for a moment where all three are now adults. They're full-fledged grown-ups now, all in their twenties—it's still an incredible thing for my mama heart to say. Wow. As I write this, Jordan has just turned twenty-six. I had a session with one of my healers a few days after his birthday because I was feeling exhausted. My body was tired the way one has aches when they have been carrying too much.

My healer told me that Jordan was in my energy field. It made perfect sense that he would be there—and as a mother, I subconsciously allowed it since I wanted to protect and embrace him, regardless of him being 26 years old. I think most mothers feel this way, especially if their child has a behavioral, emotional, or mental health challenge. I didn't even know that this energy hacking was a thing; that others could be in our energy field this way, literally piggy backing off of our energy.

My healer told me that Jordan can feel my energetic protection, that in his own way he embraced it. Allowing him to linger in my field created a cozy place for him and it appeased me, but I need to consider that it will not help him the most. She explained that I needed to release him from my energy and allow him to walk his journey.

This statement hurt my heart on so many levels, but intellectually I understood that an important part of parenting is knowing how to let go and when that helps your child to grow. She reminded me that we were not cutting the energetic ties of love and that made me feel a lot better. I finally agreed with her that this was necessary and that I must do what is best for both of us. I gave her permission to cut the energetic ties between me and Jordan, to "un-merge" Jordan from my energy field.

I realized that I had felt drained—not in the way of one who has been moving heavy boxes, but in the way of one who is pregnant or breastfeeding. Suddenly my body felt exhausted in the distinct way a mother's body tires. Obviously, I wasn't carrying and nourishing Jordan anymore. My children were now adults doing those things for themselves but this wasn't simply the jolt a mother feels when her children have left the nest... This was another kind of messaging from the Universe.

I was starting to understand that as an adult, Jordan subconsciously resented that I was inviting him to lean on me. To him it might have felt that I was implying that he couldn't do things on his own. That was not my intention, of course, but I realized how fully Jordan needed to feel that his path was his own.

As soon as I reflected on this reality, I understood it was essential for me to cut this energetic cord. I needed to commit myself to empowering my children, even if that meant future moments of accepting things I had a hard time with, like distance and separation. Jordan had a deep-soul knowing that he could live within his own circumstances and choices, and I needed to catch up.

Cutting our energetic cord was a gift I needed to give to him as well as myself. This is something we all need to do, for our own good and for our children. Cord cutting does NOT sever the love we have for our children or the love they have for us. It deepens our trust and enhances our forward momentum. We need to keep reminding ourselves, as parents and as caretakers, that bonds of love are not threatened by independence.

THE SENSITIVITY EXERCISES

Exercise One: Begin to understand your sensitivity.

Discovering how sensitive you or your child are can be a crucial step in recognizing how sensory experiences shape your daily life and emotional well-being. Sensitivities to physical and intuitive senses influence how we perceive, process, and respond to the world around us. Some individuals are naturally more attuned to subtle stimuli, like faint smells, sounds, or emotional undercurrents, while others may remain unaffected by the same environment.

This self-test is designed to help you gain insight into your or your child's level of sensitivity. By identifying these traits, you can better understand how they impact your mental and emotional health, paving the way for greater self-awareness and support. This self-test will help you gain insight into the level of sensitivity you or your child experience. Read through the following statements and note which ones reflect your or your child's experiences.

- Emotional Intensity: feeling emotions deeply and strongly, often becoming overwhelmed by them.

- Empathy: easily picking up on others' emotions and feeling them as if they were your own.

- Empathic Burnout: feeling drained or exhausted after being around others, particularly in emotionally charged situations.

- Sensory Sensitivity: being highly aware of and sensitive to sensory input such as bright lights, loud noises, or strong smells.

- Overstimulation: feeling overwhelmed or drained in busy or chaotic environments.

- Need for Alone Time: craving solitude to recharge and recover from social or sensory stimulation.

- Attention to Detail: noticing subtleties that others may overlook, such as changes in environment or people's moods.

- Creativity: having a rich inner world and often expressing yourself through creative outlets like art, music, or writing.

- Avoidance of Conflict: disliking and avoiding confrontation.

- Strong Intuition: having a keen sense of intuition and gut feelings that are often accurate.

- Physical Symptoms: experiencing physical manifestations of stress or emotional distress, such as headaches, stomachaches, or muscle tension.

- Depth of Processing: processing information deeply, often needing time to reflect before making decisions or forming opinions.

- High Emotional Reactivity: reacting strongly to both positive and negative stimuli, sometimes experiencing mood swings or intense emotional reactions.

If you found that you or your child resonated with many of the statements in the self-test, it's most likely that you or they are highly sensitive. High sensitivity is often characterized by heightened awareness of sensory input and a deep emotional or intuitive connection to the world.

While it can present challenges, such as feeling easily overwhelmed or overstimulated, it also comes with unique strengths, including creativity, empathy, and keen perception. Recognizing this trait is the first step toward understanding and embracing it, allowing you to develop strategies to nurture well-being and thrive in your sensitivity.

Exercise Two: Harness your sensitivity to find your superpower.

Being highly sensitive can often feel overwhelming, but it is also a powerful gift. Sensitivity allows you or your child to perceive the world in a unique way, and learning how to harness this awareness can lead to both personal fulfillment and a positive impact on others.

Think of an instrument designed to measure temperature, weight, pressure, or volume—we rely on its sensitivity to provide accurate and precise information. Similarly, a highly sensitive person can pick up on details and nuances that others might overlook. When used intentionally, this heightened awareness can be transformed into a source of creativity and insight.

One of the most powerful ways to channel sensitivity is through creative action, or focused attention. For example, artists and musicians use their heightened awareness of colors, sounds, and emotions to create beautiful works of art. A child who is highly sensitive might notice subtle details in music, nature, or even people's feelings, which can help them express themselves through drawing, storytelling, or playing an instrument. Sensitivity is also a valuable skill in everyday life—teachers, doctors, and caregivers use their ability to pick up on emotions and small changes to support and help others. When guided and nurtured, sensitivity can become a superpower that allows you or your child to thrive in the world.

This exercise will help you or your child tap into your innate sensitivity and channel it into a tool for inspiration, self-expression, and meaningful connection.

A. First, embrace your sensitivity.

Begin by acknowledging your sensitivity as a unique strength. Understand that it allows you to feel things more deeply, which can lead to greater creativity, intuition, and understanding. Know that your sensitivity is a wellspring of insight and inspiration waiting to be tapped into.

Affirmations can help reinforce the positive aspects of your sensitivity. Have you or your child repeat affirmations such as:

- "My sensitivity as a source of creativity and strength."

- "My emotions are a powerful fuel for my creative expression."

- "I trust my intuition and let it guide my creative journey."

B. Now channel sensitivity into creativity.

Sensitivity is deeply connected to your or child's creative energy. Rather than suppressing what you are sensing, embrace it and channel it towards you or your child's interests. Use your or your child's instincts and preferences as guides to explore new ways in which you can express your natural gifts and abilities. Experiment with different forms of expression. Art, crafts, journaling, dancing, music, acting are great outlets for expressing the full spectrum of your sensitivity. For example: If your child loves airplanes, a great way to channel their sensitivity would be spending some time on a creative project involving airplanes. The project can be as simple as building paper airplanes.

What creative action can you or your child take to channel your sensitivity in a positive way?

By reframing your sensitivity as a gift, you can use it as a source of creative energy that enhances your life and your connection to the world. This exercise will help you tap into the positive potential of your sensitivity and turn it into a tool for self-expression, personal growth, and artistic exploration.

Exercise Three: Create a soothing space to support nervous system resets.

If you or someone in your family is highly sensitive, overstimulating environments can feel overwhelming and draining. Having a dedicated space in your home for relaxation and restoration can be incredibly helpful for calming the nervous system and allowing space for peace and rest. Below are some suggestions for creating an environment that supports relaxation and helps sensitive individuals feel grounded and at ease.

A. Soft Lighting

Bright, harsh lights can overstimulate the nervous system, especially flickering lights or blue light from electronic devices. Opt for soft, warm-toned lighting, such as yellow or orange hues, which are gentler on the eyes. Salt lamps, for example, offer a soothing glow and have a calming effect on the energy in the room, helping to create a more peaceful atmosphere.

B. Calming Colors

Bright, contrasting colors can heighten sensory overload. To promote a sense of calm, choose neutral or soft colors for your space, such as gentle whites, pastels, or earth tones. Incorporating plants is another effective way to create a soothing environment. Not only do plants add calming greenery, but they also release oxygen and help purify the air, fostering a sense of connection to nature and restoring balance to the space.

C. Gentle Textures

Sensitive individuals are often very attuned to the textures of clothing, blankets, or cushions. Choose soft, natural, and comforting fabrics for bedding, pillows, and cushions that feel gentle against the skin. Fabrics like cotton, linen, hemp or silk can create a cozy, inviting space that encourages relaxation and comfort.

D. Soothing Sounds

While silence can be restorative, a busy mind may benefit from calming sounds. Play nature sounds, like flowing water or birdsong, or consider gentle music such as singing bowls, meditation tracks, or soft instrumental tunes. Try to avoid the noisy hum of electronics, which can add unnecessary stimulation and hinder relaxation. Instead, focus on sounds that are gentle and easy to listen to.

E. Calming Scents

Aromatherapy can have a powerful impact on the nervous system. Consider using a diffuser with calming essential oils such as lavender, chamomile, bergamot, frankincense, or sandalwood. These soothing scents can promote relaxation and help the body unwind. Additionally, scents like rose, sage, and patchouli can support grounding and bring a sense of comfort to the space.

F. Limiting EMF Exposure

Electromagnetic fields (EMFs) from electronic devices can contribute to nervous system overstimulation and interfere with the body's natural ability to relax. To create a more soothing environment, consider reducing exposure to EMFs by turning off electronics when not in use, especially at night. For added peace, unplug devices like routers, cell phones, and computers, or move them to another room if possible. You might also consider using EMF shielding products, such as special covers for phones or routers, to minimize electromagnetic radiation in your space. By reducing EMF exposure, you allow your nervous system to reset more easily and create a calming environment free from excessive energy interference.

By creating a space with these elements, you help provide a sanctuary for sensitive individuals, giving them a chance to reset their nervous system. This environment can offer relief from overstimulation and become a place of calm for the body, mind, and spirit.

Exercise Four: Practice clearing and protection meditations.

For highly sensitive individuals, it is very important to learn ways to clear and protect their energy field from their environment's stimuli, other people's emotions, and negative energies.

You can use the clearing meditation when you or your child feels overstimulated, overwhelmed, or heavy. You can use the protection meditation daily to shield you or your child's energy for a greater sense of peace and lightness.

If you are practicing these meditations for yourself, focus on connecting with your breath and becoming aware of your body as you follow the guided meditations. If you are doing them on behalf of your child, connect to your breathing and visualize your child throughout the meditation process, using your imagination to connect to your child's energy.

These meditations are available on the website. You may find it helpful to listen to them to assist you in the process of visualization.

Clearing Meditation

Gently close your eyes. Begin to notice the natural rhythm of your breath as it moves through your body. Take a slow, deep breath in, guiding it all the way to the base of your spine. As you inhale, imagine this breath energizing and expanding the base of your spine. On your exhale, visualize any tension or heaviness releasing from this area. With each inhale, invite in space and light. With each exhale, let go of any density or heaviness, continuing this cycle until you feel a sense of lightness and ease.

Shift your attention to the area just below your belly button. Breathe deeply into this space, visualizing your inhales filling it with light and openness. Notice any tension or heaviness in that area of your body. On each exhale, gently release any energy that no longer serves you. Let the inhales bring healing and spaciousness, and the exhales carry away the heaviness. Continue this breath until you sense lightness and harmony within.

Now bring your focus to the center of your body. Breathe deeply into this area, allowing your inhales to expand your lower ribs, infusing it with fresh air and life. On your exhales, imagine releasing any tension, heaviness, or stuck energy from this space. Let your breath flow naturally, softening and opening this area until you feel a sense of release and balance.

Turn your attention to your heart, the center of your chest. Begin to breathe deeply into this space, letting each inhale expand your chest gently and fully. With each exhale, imagine your breath massaging your heart, melting away any tension or tightness. Welcome the spaciousness and love that come with each inhale. On your exhales, let go of any negative feelings that do not serve you. Continue this breathing until you feel a sense of love and connection filling your heart.

Bring your awareness to your throat. Feel your breath as it moves in and out of this area. With every inhale, breathe in a sense of spaciousness and flow. With every exhale, release any heaviness or tension that does not align with your true essence. Continue this cycle of breathing until your throat feels clear, open, and light.

Now, direct your focus to your third eye, the center of your forehead. Visualize your breath flowing in and out of this space. As you inhale, draw in clarity, light, and insight. With each exhale, let go of any darkness or confusion clouding your perspective. Continue breathing this way until you feel a sense of clarity.

Lastly, bring your attention to the top of your head. Imagine your breath moving gently in and out of this space, opening and expanding your crown. As you inhale, visualize connecting to a boundless, unconditional source of love and light. With each exhale, release any resistance, allowing this connection to deepen. Feel your connection to love and light grow stronger with each breath.

When you're ready, take a moment to notice the lightness and spaciousness throughout your body. Slowly return your awareness to the present moment, carrying this renewed energy with you as you move through your day.

Protection Meditation

Begin by closing your eyes. Take a deep breath in, and slowly exhale, allowing yourself to settle into the present moment. Repeat this breathing cycle until you feel connected to your body.

Now, visualize a brilliant pillar of light descending from the sky, entering the top of your head through your crown chakra. Feel this pure, warm, and radiant light flowing gently yet powerfully down through the center of your body.

As this light moves downward, it illuminates each part of your being, cleansing and energizing your body, mind, and spirit. See it flowing through your head, throat, heart, and solar plexus, down to your lower abdomen, and finally to the base of your spine.

From the base of your spine, envision the light traveling deep into the earth, grounding you and connecting you to the nurturing energy of Mother Earth. Feel a sense of stability and support rising from this connection.

Now, see this pillar of light expand outward, filling your entire body with its radiant glow. Let it grow even further, extending past your physical form, creating a luminous sphere of white diamond light around you. This bubble sparkles brilliantly, impenetrable and pure, surrounding you in a protective cocoon of light.

Feel the loving presence of this luminous light shielding you from all energies, emotions, or influences that do not serve your highest good. Trust in this light's unwavering protection.

As you bask in this protective light, bring your awareness to your heart. Feel a profound sense of gratitude for the Source of Unconditional Love, Light, and Protection that is always available to you. Let this gratitude radiate from your heart, filling your entire being and extending outward into the universe.

When you are ready, take a few deep breaths, gently wiggle your fingers and toes, and open your eyes, carrying this sense of protection and peace with you throughout your day.

3

THE ART OF STILLNESS

(see also: calm, noiselessness, serenity)

Monarch butterflies will not attempt to fly in rain storms because the raindrops will damage their wings. They rest through the heavy weather and wait in stillness for storms to pass. This is called self-preservation. It's okay to rest during the storms in your life. It's okay to wait, knowing that you will fly again beautifully when the storm has passed.

Why do people treat solitude like a bad word? Often the most productive, beautiful choice is resting, giving yourself sometime to disconnect and recharge. Remember that we are human-beings not human-doings.

There are thousands of books and videos out there telling us to make better or different choices regarding food, exercise, and meditation. Only you can find what works for you. And what works for you will change and evolve over time. This is all so individual—there's no sense in any self-help author or guru pretending it's a one-size-fits-all scenario. (My grandfather used to see garments in his retail store marked one-size-fits-all and he would respond by saying "one size fits none!") But here's a thing that is true for us all, and I think it's sacred: your body is designed to protect you. That's why it's essential that we keep seeking our well-being, we keep reducing stress, and we keep bringing peace to our daily lives.

His Holiness the Dalai Lama once said that if we teach every eight-year-old child how to meditate we will eliminate violence from the world in one generation. Study after study shows that people who meditate lower their risk of anxiety, hypertension, high cholesterol, adult onset diabetes, and more. And I can tell you, anecdotally, you're less likely to scream in the school carpool drop-off line!

Before my manic episode and spiritual awakening, I was never able to sit still. When my brother recommended that I do yoga, I laughed at him and said that I didn't have time for it. I realize now it's the people that say that they don't have time for yoga or meditation that need it the most! It would not have killed me to take the time to stand in *tadasana* (tree pose) or in *matyasana* (fish pose), or even to lie in *Shavasana* (corpse pose). In fact, it would have centered me!

In hindsight, I realize that I had undiagnosed anxiety and PTSD from my early childhood trauma. I think I always kept busy because I was too scared to slow down and look within. I thought that if I had a thousand things to do, the past was never going to catch up with me. It's amazing to me, and shocking to my lifelong friends that I am now able to sit down and relax, that meditation is now a yummy part of my life. However, it has taken me a looong time to get to this state to truly experience rest and relaxation.

Medication is one way to help us slow down. However, there are also ways to help us calm our nervous systems and be able to relax naturally. Going to the root cause of what is causing us to be, let's say, over-energetic, can be transformational and have life-long benefits. We will talk more about this in Chapter Seven: The Art of Healing.

I was speaking with a client, Jeff, who told me that he asked his wife if she could please be nice to him for a 24-hour period. To his surprise, she said no. I was especially shocked when I found out that she was a mindfulness teacher. What was I missing? Was this an exercise in authenticity for Jeff's wife, or was she a woman who, no matter what her profession, was at her wit's end? I spoke to a therapist friend about this. She told me that when we react, we are actually acting from our subconscious mind. Our hurt inner child gets triggered; and usually we are not consciously aware that we are being triggered, or what these triggers are. Jeff had been hurt by his wife's answer and now they are in couples therapy.

What else could help them? This is where I questioned if meditation was enough to reverse negative behaviors. Maybe additional work needed to be done to see where this wound—or these wounds—originated from. Can we work toward removing the layers of pain surrounding the hurt in order to heal it? Jeff was willing to consider multiple modalities. His path to healing is still a work in progress, but the key thing is that he's on the path toward healing and positivity. Whether or not they will stay together and be happy is yet to be seen.

There is no schedule for healing and there is no perfect age to do it. Just like there is no perfect age to fall in love, to go back to school, to try a new sport, or start a new career. You are not behind in life. That's simply not possible. You do not need to rush—you're not late. You are exactly where you are supposed to be! It's up to the Universe how long things take, not us, so push away any frantic feelings you have about getting this healing thing done.

It's a lifelong journey; a continuing education. One of my healers recently told me that the Universe is our school and we are here to learn, to keep growing with the end goal of becoming one with our higher selves.

In this life you are allowed to take breaks.

You are allowed to linger—lingering is not languishing.

You are allowed stillness.

When our daughter Rachel was twelve years old, she was diagnosed with Graves' disease. Graves' disease is an autoimmune disorder that can cause hyperthyroidism, or overactive thyroid. Common signs and symptoms of Graves' disease include anxiety and irritability, little tremors in your hands or fingers, weight loss despite healthy eating habits, change in menstrual cycles, bulging eyes, fatigue and sleep disturbances. Rachel had most of these symptoms.

Prior to her diagnosis, Rachel had been playing competitive softball. Travel softball at this level had been a significant commitment for a 7th grader. As her symptoms emerged, due to Rachel's age and the pressure she was under as an athlete, doctors immediately had fears about an eating disorder, but that wasn't really what was going on. Rachel agreed to take medication for her Grave's disease, but she refused to take medicine for her newly formed anxiety and depression.

She had also refused to see a therapist, but started working with a Reiki practitioner and other healers. Soon she was training with a female shaman. That was when her own healing gifts began to emerge. Rachel is able to actually see traumas stuck in her clients bodies. She guides her clients to release these traumas from a new and restorative emotional place. In this way she is able to transmute what she calls "yuck" from the body and replace it with "yum."

Rachel is a sensitive being who I believe is the epitome of an empath. In her young adult life, with all she experiences, she believes that everything is healable. I'm so grateful for her point of view, which has been a guiding light for me and she has taught me so much. It has been quite the journey to watch her transform her challenges into gifts; to see how deeply mindful she is; how she is able to help others with her gifts. She has recently been given the spiritual name Louru. Watching her medically-trained father embrace her spiritual gifts has been nothing short of a miracle to observe.

Something essential I learned in meditation is that stillness prepares us to receive. Often, we don't know what we are about to receive, whether it is calm, wisdom, inspiration, or spiritual guidance. Anticipation isn't the point; openness is. There is a saying that when we pray, we speak to God. When we meditate, we listen to God. The goal is to quiet our minds enough to be able to hear that inner voice that comes from a place of unconditional love. If there is negativity or anything aside from unconditional love, then it isn't God's voice. This was a HUGE lesson that I needed to learn. When I think that my inner voice is rushing me to do something or is making me anxious, then it is not from God. And boy oh boy, does the darkness like to act like God.

What if something you've been praying for is about to happen for you? You've been patient, you've remained strong through trials and challenges. Nothing has broken you— you had doubts, but you were ultimately able to access your inner strength, to stand firm in your truth. Maybe now is the time for you to start receiving. Let's allow ourselves to believe the Universe has a plan for us and it's a good one!

THE STILLNESS EXERCISES

We live in a culture that prioritizes productivity and constant activity. However, our nervous system is not designed to remain in a perpetual state of alertness. To maintain long-term physical and mental well-being, it is essential to cultivate moments of deep rest and stillness, allowing the body to shift into a state of relaxation. In this state, vital functions such as digestion, immunity, regeneration, and cellular repair take priority, supporting overall health and balance.

Finding the most restorative practices for yourself may require some exploration. Here are a few activities that can help calm the nervous system and promote relaxation:

- Yoga

- Meditation

- Breathing techniques

- Chanting or humming

- Spending time in nature

- Tai Chi

- Qi Gong

- Sound baths

By incorporating these practices into your routine, you can support your body's natural ability to restore and heal.

Breath and Body Awareness Meditation

This practice can be as brief as a few minutes or as long as several hours. If you're new to meditation, start with a few minutes and gradually extend your sessions to twenty minutes a day.

Let go of expectations about results or how long you can maintain focus—clarity will come naturally with time and practice. The most important thing is to keep returning to your practice, again and again.

Find a comfortable seated position, allowing your spine to lengthen naturally. Gently close your eyes. Relax your jaw and shoulders, softening any tension in your posture.

Bring your attention to your breath. Notice where you feel it most clearly—perhaps in your chest, your belly, or as a subtle sensation on your upper lip, where the air moves in and out just below your nostrils. Observe your breath with a neutral mind and a relaxed body.

It is natural for the mind to wander. Whenever you notice your attention drifting, simply and gently return your focus to your breath—without judgment. Cultivate a sense of neutrality, allowing each moment to unfold as it is.

Now shift your focus to sensations within your body. Select one sensation—perhaps warmth, tingling, or pressure—and observe it with curiosity. If your mind drifts, gently guide it back to the sensations unfolding in the present. For the next several moments, notice how sensations may change over time, and continue to observe them without resistance or attachment.

Slowly bring your attention back to your breath. Allow your breath to become deeper and fuller, awakening your body. When you feel ready, open your eyes, bringing your attention back into the room.

Nervous System Reset and Deep Relaxation Meditation

Find a comfortable position, either seated or lying down. Gently close your eyes and bring your attention to your breath. Notice the natural rise and fall of your inhales and exhales, allowing each breath to anchor you into the present moment.

Start building a deeper breath, allowing your exhales to be twice as long as your inhales. Let each breath be smooth and effortless. These extended exhales signal to your nervous system that it is safe to relax, shifting you into a state of calm.

Let's build on these deeper breaths, taking your inhales to a count of three and your exhales to a count of six, if possible. Start by emptying your lungs. Inhale deeply through your nose for a count of three-two-one, then slowly exhale through your mouth for a count of six-five-four-three-two-one.

Repeat this cycle at your pace for five more breaths.

Now, release the structured breath count and allow your breathing to settle into a natural rhythm. With each inhale, imagine a wave of calming energy flowing through your body, nourishing every cell. With each exhale, feel yourself releasing any tension, letting go of heaviness from your muscles, bones, and organs.

Rest in this deep state of relaxation for as long as you'd like, allowing your nervous system to fully reset. When you're ready to return, take a slow, deep breath in and exhale completely. Wiggle your fingers and toes, and gently open your eyes, carrying this sense of calm with you.

This practice can be done anytime you need to reset and restore. The more consistently you practice, the more easily your nervous system will return to balance.

4

THE ART OF INTUITION

(see also: instinct, divination, inspiration)

I love how this chapter immediately follows the chapter on stillness (thank you Stacy, my magical editor)! Being still helps us to quiet our minds and get in touch with our inner knowing, also known as our intuition. The Merriam-Webster definition of intuition is "the power of knowing immediately and without conscious reasoning." I never knew the true meaning of this word before my spiritual awakening. I always heard about a mother's gifts of her sixth sense or her gut knowing. However, I never understood what this was and that this is a real thing!

We all have a gift from the Universe known as our gut instinct (which can also be considered a form of intuition). The problem is that we don't always listen to our intuition because our monkey brains get in the way. Listening to our intuition feels very calm and peaceful. As opposed to the anxious, fearful emotions we feel when our conscious mind gets in the way.

Many of us have traumas and dramas from our childhood that prevent us from feeling calm and safe. This can decrease our ability to listen to our intuition. There are several healing modalities that help shift our bodies from fight or flight into the parasympathetic realm, allowing us to calmly listen to our divine guidance.

There are other ways to obtain divine guidance in addition to meditating and listening to our intuition. Applied kinesiology, for example, allows practitioners to work with patients to select appropriate treatments by testing muscles for strength and weakness. Chiropractors often use this to manually muscle test their patients. I have learned several ways to do muscle testing which helps me and my clients in obtaining guidance from our higher selves. We ALL have access to our subconscious minds and this has been transformational for me when I am not able to tell the difference between my intuition and my conscious mind.

I have met so many people recently whose backgrounds vary tremendously. Some believe in a higher power, some do not. Some think that God is an external existence while others believe that it is a voice within us. I was invited to join a Fearless Women's Group which includes Bible study. (I am Jewish so some of this is new for me as Jewish folks do not utilize the New Testament). What I love most about this group is that the women talk about "God-winks" and sometimes start discussions by saying "God said to me . . . " It's incredible. Imagine we are living in a world where we have a direct connection to our Creator and either hear him directly or receive lessons from the Universe—messages that you know are from a Higher Source?

For me, not knowing that there was a Higher Power for the first 48 years of my life, you can only imagine how much fear, anxiety and pressure I felt. It was as if I had the burden of the world sitting on my shoulders. That is too much for anyone to handle, especially when you are raising a gifted and challenging child.

Even though many of my friends and clients have a belief and/or relationship with a Higher Power, it amazes me that they still experience fear and anxiety. I have learned that there are two ways of existing in the world, fear vs faith. And that we cannot live in both at the same time. Imagine a world where there was less fear, anxiety, anger, shame, blame and guilt and more peace, faith, love and trust. Our world would be a much better place. That is what I call Heaven on Earth.

In the exercise section at the end of this chapter we will share with you a method for muscle testing, a form of kinesiology. One of the MOST important things to note is that it is imperative to do a protection prayer before you do the testing to keep the darkness out and from mis-guiding us. I'll say more on this type of protection later. Again, the key is to keep an open mind.

Over time, I noticed how my husband's stresses, just like my anxieties, were affecting Jordan. Once I realized this, I was determined to do whatever I could to move us all from a place of fear and anxiety towards greater peace, with greater emphasis on faith, love and trust. As Harvard psychologist Dr. Craig Malkin reminds us, an essential part of change is opening up to new ways of relating.

My next goal was to encourage my husband to heal and shift, not only for our health as a couple, but because of the positive effect it would have on Jordan. Some of you are married or in partnerships of your own and saying, "Uh-oh, no way, Mara." So, allow me to specify that I wasn't setting out to change him. I was only trying to help him feel better and shift the energy in our home and in our family life.

I will never forget the day that my husband, my daughter and I were getting ready to go on a trip. My husband's neurosis about flying was on full display when he wanted us to leave for the airport three hours earlier than necessary. I told him that he was crazy; he told me that I was self-centered.

I was not about to let his *mishigas* ruin the travel day for me and our daughter. I was grateful when Rachel said to Kenny, "Why don't you go to the airport now. Mom and I will meet you there?" He begrudgingly said no and waited for us. Mind you, this was not a victory. He was Mr. Cranky Pants the entire time. He didn't chill out until we were actually sitting on the airplane. Literally!

When we returned home from our trip, I told Kenny that this was no way for us to live. I begged him—well in reality, I insisted he do this—to go with me to see one of my healers. He finally agreed. On the drive there, Kenny kept saying that this was stupid. I managed to bite my tongue, took deep Piggie Bear belly breaths, letting him bitch and complain. When we arrived at the hypnotherapist's office, I actually said a prayer in my head, begging for this to work and for Kenny to actually go through with it.

We got in the elevator and I pushed floor number four. As the door opened, the hypnotherapist was standing there to welcome us with a big, warm smile. I thought to myself, there is no turning back now. We walked into the office, and of course I started speaking because Kenny had a hard time admitting that there was an issue. He used to try to reason with me by saying "I am perfect" and I thought to myself, silly man, no one is perfect! That is why we are here on University of Planet Earth, to learn, grow, and heal. (Let's all swap "I need to be perfect" with "I am human.")

And then the moment came, the hypnotherapist asked Kenny to stand up. He guided him through a clearing; the magic began. Mr. C performed a technique he called biofeedback; it's a type of muscle testing using the person's body to access their subconscious mind. It's similar to kinesiology where you ask the body a question and it gives a yes/no answer.

Mr. C asked four types of questions to ascertain if Kenny was holding emotional, physical, cellular or spiritual emotions and trauma. It's amazing. The body actually sways backwards or forwards to represent yes/no answers. I could see that Kenny's breathing was rapid and that his body was stiff at first. But after the first few questions, he began to relax and his breathing became slower.

Biofeedback, or this type of kinesiology, is a technique that can be used to obtain answers from the subconscious mind. The idea behind biofeedback is that harnessing the power of your subconscious can help reveal what emotions are being trapped in our sub-conscious mind. Biofeedback supports us in letting go of negative emotions and helps free us from the things that are keeping us from living our full potential.

Mr. C was able to discover that Kenny took on energy from one of his parents that caused his anxiety about traveling. When he asked Kenny if he was ready to release it, Kenny responded yes! And voila, just like that, Kenny's anxiety about being late disap-peared. Of course, I had to see this to believe it myself. A week later we were meeting friends for dinner and for the first time Kenny was not pacing around the bedroom anx-iously waiting for me to be ready. The peace that came out of this had a direct, positive impact on Jordan because as an empath, Jordan felt both of our anxieties. With us feeling calmer, Jordan was able to experience the same.

The real magic occurred when we prepared for our next airplane trip. Kenny was more relaxed about us leaving for the airport. Soon Kenny started sharing with his patients the story of his transformation. To my surprise, he began referring patients to our HUGS Healing Center, which consists of a team of vetted, holistic healers that offer healing modalities that complement Western medicine.

I had created this organization as a result of the positive effects my healers had on my life, my families, my friends and my clients. I knew that I needed to share them and their healing modalities with the world! Kenny shared with his patients that he did not understand how his healing occurred, but that he felt like a new person because of it. What better way to bridge the gap between medical professionals and holistic healers than with testimonies from a Western trained medical physician?

When working in Kenny's OB/GYN office, I was able to see transformations that took place with patients who saw our healers. I noticed that the types of patients the Universe sent to see Dr. Kenny was changing. He became the perfect OB/GYN to help guide his patients to shift their fears and anxiety. His new patients included women who suffered PTSD from their past deliveries, or lived with excessive amounts of fear, anxiety, and depression. Several patients admitted that they could not get through the day without taking pills. They were pleased to have possible new solutions for their health, grateful that their OB/GYN was truly listening and taking an open-minded approach to their concerns and offering alternative solutions.

Clearing negative emotions and unspoken fears from mothers and mothers-to-be can have a direct, positive impact for their children. According to the United Nations Committee on the Rights of the Child (CRC), understanding and prioritizing the mental health of mothers is crucial. A mother's stability directly influences her child's positive psychological and emotional growth. In providing supportive and nurturing environments for themselves as well as their babies, mothers create solid foundations for their children's futures.

As the saying goes, there are many roads to Rome. This is true with parenting as well. There is no one correct way to parent, which makes it an even more difficult endeavor. Our gut tells us one thing and our mind tells us another. It is often hard to judge which one to follow.

Just the other day, my daughter was asking me questions about why I did things in certain, specific ways when she was younger. She prefaced her questions with "I don't want you to feel guilty…" so I knew this was not going to be the easiest of conversations.

She wanted to know why I had locked her in her room one night when she was only six years old. I shared with her that a therapist Kenny and I were working with spoke to us about empowering our children vs. enabling them and how that idea had instilled fear in me. I did not yet know what it meant to parent from the heart, to do so out of love instead of fear. I thought that I was doing the right thing that night. I thought I needed to be more tough and firm. I'm shocked now and mortified that I did such a thing to my baby girl.

So years later, I saw it— how she was still impacted by that occurrence. I apologized and told her how sorry I was. I had acted out of pure fear instead of acting from my love for her. She asked me "Why didn't you lock your door instead of locking me inside of my room." Wow! I wanted to go back to our old therapist who instructed me to do this but what good would that do now? I needed to release my guilt and know that I did what I did based on what I knew then, even though I didn't follow my heart. These days, I tell my clients to trust their hearts, to trust their instincts, but I had not been good at telling myself those things back then.

I cannot undo what I have done in the past. But it's never too late to do better; to begin parenting differently. I can share my experiences, the lessons I have learned. I am tempted to say to you that I am not an expert. Friends remind me not to do that. They keep reminding me that women with lived experiences are the experts. It's rewarding and humbling to hear.

I hope readers will learn from my mistakes. My very wise 21-year-old daughter has helped me realize that my husband and I often parented from a place of fear. Thankfully she understands that we are human, that we have always loved her very much and feel pain that there were moments she believed the opposite was true. Parenting takes devotion, training, and endurance. I am reminded again and again that it is a marathon, not a sprint.

There is a newish buzz around conscious parenting. This is also known as peaceful parenting and various other terms. Conscious parenting is about letting go of a parent's ego, desires, and attachments. Instead of forcing behaviors on children, parents are supposed to focus on their own language, their expectations, and their self-regulation. When I was raising my children, I never heard of the term conscious parenting and if I did, I am not even sure that I would have fully understood the devotion and mindfulness it required.

According to acclaimed clinical psychologist and bestselling author Dr. Shefali Tsabary (popularly known as Dr. Shefali), "To parent unconsciously means to be unaware that as a parent, we are carrying emotional baggage. When we parent unconsciously, just presuming that we are the greater than, we know more, because we are just older, this is where mishaps happen and this is where we create a dysfunction within the parental child relationship." She goes on to say that "to enter a conscious state of parenting and of awareness means to understand that our emotional imprints that we inherited from our parents is going to directly impact and bear upon the parental relationship that we have with our child."

Dr. Shefali points out that if we fail to take this into supreme consideration we will miss the fact that when our child acts out it's our energy that is in there as well; that when a child has a problem, it's our energetic imprint that is in that mix and this is what she sees happening over and over again, a failing of the parent to understand their own baggage in the relationship, they just divorce themselves from the problem and now only the child is the problem and when the child begins to grow up, they feel that they are carrying the burden of everyone's problems.

The first step for us to parent our children consciously or peacefully is to be able to humble ourselves and this is no easy feat. We cannot consciously parent when we have a hurt inner child that subconsciously reacts and interferes with our parenting. I have a client who meditates and practices gratitude and says positive affirmations daily. However, when it comes to her husband and children, she finds herself reacting and is not able to take a mindful moment to collect herself.

I was perplexed by this behavior. I asked a colleague about it. She shared with me that meditation works on the conscious mind. Our reactions and automated responses occur from our subconscious mind. This is why it's so important to work on healing and re-parenting our own inner child to positively affect our subconscious mind.

Reparenting ourselves helps us to shed our jaded lenses; to see our children for who they are and not who we want them to be. We are then able to parent our children from a place of unconditional love—not fear, or issues of control. It is so important for a parent to realize and understand that our children are NOT a reflection of us. They reflect to us the things we need to heal. I cannot say this enough. It is an essential lesson.

It is good for us to analyze the family baggage and conditioning that we have been raised with in order for us to free ourselves from placing these upon our children. However, I have noticed with clients over and over again, that they do not consciously remember negative moments that they experienced as a young child.

Many of my clients say "I had a great childhood!" I respond by telling them that might be the case, but there might have been a time in their childhood that their parents or someone else didn't act in the best interest for their wellbeing. Then I tell them that it doesn't matter what they uncover because look at how amazing they turned out to be today!

I share with my clients about my childhood and that I didn't remember my childhood trauma until I was 52 years old, and let me tell you, it was beyond traumatic. In hindsight, having this memory was an important step in my personal healing journey. Seeing the positive effects that my healing journey had on my children, especially Jordan, has been profound and what parent wouldn't do anything and everything to help their child?

I am now grateful to be living with a strong sense of peace, faith, love, and trust. It took a beautiful yet rude spiritual awakening—and *a lot*, I mean A LOT of healing—to be where I am today. I feel forever grateful that my life has taken this turn for the better. There is way too much fear, anger and anxiety in our lives. To be able to give this over to a Higher Power and know that I am not alone has been a true blessing to me and can be for you too!

When children are diagnosed with an emotional or mental health challenge, I rarely if ever hear the medical world talk about the child being an empath. This, as we discussed in chapter two, means that they actually "feel" the energy and emotions of those around them. I wish that I knew this when my children were younger because I can only imagine what they felt when they were near me, an anxious neurotic mother and my husband, an energized and anxious father.

When I started my first podcast series, *Let's Talk Wellness*, I interviewed an amazing array of doctors, community advocates, and healers. If I had not experienced all of these healing modalities first-hand and swear by them, I would not feel so committed to sharing these discussions with others. It took quite a lot to truly open my mind, to see the world differently, and to appreciate the Universe. I want others to be able to experience the healing and nurturing part—without having manic episodes of their own.

My subsequent podcast, *Beyond the Symptoms*, has allowed me to continue healing and enter into a new era of learning. If we want to move the dial on mental health challenges and help people suffer less, we need to begin looking at complementary healing modalities, energy work, even past life regression therapies. I would not present these practices if I had not had truly positive experiences proving their value. It has been my honor to witness meaningful transformations for friends, family, and clients that could not have been achieved by medication and talk therapy alone. These life changes required non-traditional healing modalities plus a willingness or curiosity to learn more.

Coming from a family of Western-trained medical professionals—my older son recently became the 7th OB-GYN in my husband's family—including my father the dentist and my brother the physician, I never imagined I would be here today writing about holistic healing and encouraging my friends and family towards new healing modalities. I founded the HUGS Healing Center to help introduce people to amazing, vetted healers who help people improve in the way they face mental and emotional challenges. They do this in a way that complements Western medicine yet expands our idea of healing and healthcare.

Within HUGS, my colleagues and I wanted others to be open to the connection between mental health and spirituality. Our healers at the HUGS Healing Center help clients reach new perspectives by uncovering the emotions underlying their mental and physical ailments. I've started to refer to these as "dis-eases." (See what I did there?!) But seriously, what if we could ease the pressure we put on ourselves; what if we could ease the fear we feel, or the negativity we may not even realize is affecting us? So we work to make holistic healing accessible to more people. Recently I heard a young woman refer to Reiki as "something my wealthy aunt does." It doesn't have to be that way. We should all have access to the expert healers we need.

More than anything I urge you to be open to the possibilities—meaning I want you to try every modality that grabs your attention—it is a great gift to find something new to help you live a happier, healthier life that you might not have even thought was possible.

Are you ready for one of my golden rules? Here it is: never say "no" to your children.

I can see you mamas out there with dropping jaws and raised eyebrows, but I'm serious. The word no has a certain sorcery with children. Once they hear it they go into offense-defense mode and there is no winning at this stage. But let me clarify. This does not mean that you say yes to your child, this simply means you avoid the word no.

For example, if your child wants to go get ice-cream, instead of a simple no, you might say, "That's not going to work into our schedule right now, but maybe we could go after school on Wednesday or Thursday." Technically of course the answer is still no, but you're validating their idea and keeping open the line of communication.

A client called yesterday and said that her thirteen-year-old had asked to get her nose pierced. She broke the golden rule and immediately said no, at which point her daughter freaked out. We discussed her possible responses when her child asks again, because I imagine her child will be as persistent as mine were in these instances. It's tempting to say something like "When you're older, we'll discuss it." If your child is smart like mine (and occasionally wise asses, lol) they might say something like, "Okay, I'm five minutes older now, let's discuss." You may want to answer with precision. "Let's revisit this discussion on or after your eighteenth birthday."

It's also a fine time to seek more information. "I didn't know this was something that interested you. How long have you wanted one? Do people you admire have them? Does it bother you that it might hurt?"

The thing is, we expect positivity from our kids but it's possible they hear negative answers too often and in a way that discourages their agency and confidence; their independent, creative thinking; as well as their own strengthening instincts and intuition. Removing "no" from our parent vocabulary can have an amazing impact.

Similarly, I stopped saying "don't forget." Putting the word forget out into the world was almost like manifesting that they would indeed forget. If I said, "Don't forget to give your teacher the permission slip," the *forget* part seemed to be the part their brains took in. I started saying "please remember" instead. This is obviously a more positive notion, and if their brain clung to only one word of the instruction, it would be "remember," not forget. *Please remember to give your teacher the permission slip.*

What I mean is, it's not simply a matter of word choice. It's setting tasks and conversations in a more affirming and reassuring manner. I can hear the sceptics among you saying, does it really matter? And I promise you that putting positive energies into the world always has benefits for you and your children.

While we're adding positivity to the world (amazing!), I want to share something I heard recently. I was describing to a friend how the addition of a morning meditation to my life was transformative. She told me that morning was the best time for "habit stacking." I'm familiar with the studies that a new, beneficial habit can be formed in as few as eighteen days, although for many of us it might take sixty or more. But I hadn't heard of habit stacking, where you tie a new activity to an established one.

Let's say the basic schedule of your day is waking to your alarm, making coffee, and brushing your teeth. You eat lunch at your office, you pick up your kids, you get everyone into bed, including yourself, at a hopefully reasonable hour. Stacking new habits into this routine looks like this: Wake to your alarm/drink a full glass of water. Make coffee/take a few moments for your morning meditation. Brush teeth/say your affirmations. Lunch at the office/get outside for a ten-minute walk. Drive to get the kids/listen to a wellness podcast or audiobook. Bedtime routine/write in your gratitude journal three or four things for which you're grateful for today. And just like that you've done it—you've made additional daily care an ongoing part of your routine.

You're taking better care of you, which is guaranteed to make you a better parent.

THE INTUITION EXERCISES

Exercise One: Connecting to Your Intuition

Intuition is often described as a deep inner knowing—a sense of understanding that arises without the need for conscious reasoning. It's our gut feeling that warns us of danger, our heart pull that guides us toward an opportunity, or the quiet whisper that nudges us in the right direction. While we all have intuition, many of us have been conditioned to ignore or second-guess it, favoring logic and analysis instead.

However, intuition is not separate from intelligence—it is simply a different form of it, one that operates beyond words and calculations. This is because our intuition isn't housed in the thinking mind alone; it is deeply connected to three powerful centers of intelligence: the head, the heart, and the gut. These three centers guide our perception, decision-making, and overall experience of life. Modern neuroscience confirms what ancient wisdom traditions have long understood: in addition to our head brain, we also have an intrinsic intelligence within our heart and gut.

Each of these three centers processes information in unique ways:

- The Head Brain –The left hemisphere governs logic, reasoning, and analytical thought, while the right hemisphere governs intuition, creativity, and imagination.

- The Heart Brain – Processes emotions, intuition, and relational understanding.

- The Gut Brain – Regulates survival instincts, deep knowing, and subconscious awareness.

We tend to over-rely on our head brain, using logic and analysis to navigate life while often dismissing the wisdom of the heart and gut. When we integrate these three centers, we gain access to a deeper, more intuitive way of knowing, enhancing our ability to make decisions, connect with others, and move through life with greater ease.

The following exercise is designed to activate, align, and integrate the three brains, allowing intuition and logic to work together harmoniously. By doing so, you'll strengthen your ability to trust your instincts, listen to your heart, and think with greater clarity—all while feeling more grounded and centered.

In this exercise, we will use one of the most ancient and sacred sounds, AUM, to create a powerful resonance that aligns the gut, heart, and head, strengthening the connection between logic and intuition.

AUM it is typically considered to have three syllables:

A (pronounced like "ah")

U (pronounced like "oo")

M (pronounced like "mm")

As you chant AUM, feel its vibration moving through each brain, harmonizing your three centers and awakening a deeper sense of connection within.

A. Activate your gut center: your source of instinct and deep knowing.

Place your hands on your belly. Notice the movement of your breath in this area, deepening your breath if needed. Hum or chant **AUM** three to six times while keeping your focus on your belly.

B. Activate your heart center: your source of emotional intelligence and inner guidance.

Move your hands to your heart center. Observe how your breath moves through your chest. Hum or chant **AUM** three to six times, focusing on your heart.

C. Activate your head center: your source of logical and intuitive thought.

Place your hands on the sides of your head, just above your ears. Tune into the connection between the right and left hemispheres of your brain. Hum or chant **AUM** three to six times while holding this focus.

D. Align and integrate the three brains.

Rest your hands and bring your awareness to your natural breath. With each inhale, visualize energy flowing from your gut to your heart, and up to your head, connecting them. With each exhale, imagine a smooth pathway forming from your head, down towards your heart, and into your belly. Repeat this connected breathing for three to six cycles. You may visualize a figure-eight or infinity symbol flowing between these three centers.

This practice is a powerful way to center and ground yourself, making it an excellent preparation for meditation, journaling, or creative work. By reconnecting with your intuitive intelligence, you cultivate a deeper presence and alignment with yourself, allowing you to engage with the world more fully and confidently.

This exercise has a cumulative effect in connecting you to your intuition and expanding your brain capacity to process and respond to life. We recommend you practice it daily.

Exercise Two: Accessing Your Body's Intuitive Wisdom

Our bodies hold a deep well of wisdom—an innate intelligence that constantly communicates with us. We can access this guidance to help support our decisions, from choosing nourishing foods to making life choices that align with our highest good or the highest good for our children.

In the following exercise, you will be using a form of Applied Kinesiology or Biofeedback to access your body's innate wisdom by asking yes-or-no questions to guide you in making more aligned decisions in different areas of your life.

Before you begin, do your best to remain neutral and detached from the outcome of the answers.

A. First, establish your neutral stance.

- Stand comfortably with your feet hip-distance apart.

- Bring your awareness to the area just below your belly button, feeling your center of gravity.

- Relax your body while maintaining an upright posture, allowing yourself to feel balanced and stable.

B. Next, create a clear space.

- *Say out loud or in your head: " I connect only with information coming from my Higher Self for my highest good"*

C. Now identify your body's yes and no responses.

- From your neutral stance, say: "Body, show me YES."

- Again, stay relaxed and observe your body's response.

- Most people naturally lean forward, moving toward their center for a yes response.

- Reset to a neutral standing position, then say: "Body, show me NO."

- Stay relaxed and simply observe how your body moves.

- Most people experience a gentle backward sway, moving away from the center.

If you do not get a clear yes or no response, don't worry—this can happen for several reasons. First, check your state of mind and body. If you're feeling anxious, fatigued, or emotionally charged, take a few deep breaths to center yourself before testing again. Ensuring you're well-hydrated can also improve accuracy, as dehydration can weaken muscle responses.

If you're still unsure about your body's answers, take a break, reset your energy by grounding yourself (such as standing barefoot on the earth or practicing slow breathing), and return to the test later with a fresh perspective. Trust the process—your body's wisdom will become clearer with practice and patience.

D. Next, confirm your *yes* and *no* responses.

To ensure accuracy, test your body's responses with this simple step:

1. Stand neutrally and say: "My name is [your actual name]."
   - Observe how your body moves. It should match your *yes* response.

2. Reset to neutral, then say: "My name is Joe Schmoe" (haha)
   - Notice whether your body moves the same way it did for your *no*.

If your body responds consistently, you're ready to use it for intuitive guidance. If not, revisit the previous step.

E. Use your body for inner guidance.

Now that you've established your body's *yes* and *no* responses, you can use this technique to ask questions to access your inner wisdom:

- Hold a supplement, food, or skincare product close to your body and ask: "Body, is this beneficial for me?" Notice your body's response.

- You can also ask any questions that require a yes or no answer, such as: "Is it in my best interest to _____" or " Is it in my child's best interest to _____." Notice your body's response.

This technique can become a valuable tool for making decisions that align with your body's intuitive wisdom.

5

THE ART OF PERSPECTIVE

(see also: prospect, mindset, viewpoint)

*O*h boy, here it goes. It has taken me years of healing and trusting to be able to "come out" with this chapter. I ask you to *please* be open minded to my perspective of mental health challenges. I keep hearing my hubby and father-in-law in the back of my head as I write this chapter saying "Mara, you're crazy!" I can see them in my mind's eye giving me the look, rolling their eyes. But ever since my manic episode/spiritual awakening, *I knew absolutely* that I needed to share this with the world.

I want to call this "the truth" but I know that's not exactly right; this is *my truth*, it's for me to stand firm within, and not everyone believes the same things. We have different foundations and life experiences. Just like in religion, everyone has their own core beliefs and stands faithful to the things they were taught and raised with, their own stepping stones. I am here to give you another perspective on mental health challenges, a second or alternative path to follow if you wish.

The choices are yours of course—no matter what you decide I am grateful you are here, taking a journey with me by reading these pages. In my experience, all religions have part of the truth, whereas spirituality is the truth. Remember learning that people once believed the world was flat? Then it was explained to people that actually the world is round? It amazes me to hear there are people out there who still believe that the world is flat. As humans, we have the ability to tolerate divergent beliefs as well as the capacity to explain our own. So let's love one another for who we are, not for what we believe or don't believe. If only we could change the human experience so that we could be less judgmental and more loving and accepting. That is when I believe we will experience Heaven on Earth.

In my non-profit foundation work, people often ask me how I got started. Their faces register surprise when I say it actually began with a manic episode. I now describe my "manic month of May" as my "magical month of May." It ultimately transformed my life in a positive way. I truly believe that during my episode, I was in something like a state of spiritual enlightenment. And when the Universe, or God, or whatever you call it, tells you to do something, you do it! Ha ha.

I know that might sound over the top, but during my awakening my ego disappeared. My thoughts came from a place of pure, unconditional love. There was no chaos making noise in my head. All of my negative thoughts and dislikes vanished. There were moments I felt I was living in a state of pure bliss. While it may not be a perfect comparison, I said it was something like the happy relaxed feeling you have after a glass (or maybe a bottle!) of wine.

During this time, I was not grounded. I felt as if I was living in Nirvana, like Heaven on Earth. Once I was heavily medicated, I was brought out of this state of pure bliss. Now that I had experienced such a state, I spend time meditating to get those feelings of freedom and joy back. In that happy place there was only love and light so no one was able to push my buttons.

No one was able to agitate me, even if they wanted to. I was pure, unconditional love. Even a significant anger from the past, toward a friend who had hurt me deeply, just sort of magically disappeared. I was in a constant state of *being* v. *doing.* I lived in the here-and-now.

There is a saying that when we worry about the future, we experience anxiety. When we focus on the past, we feel depressed. Living in the here-and-now is the best place to be, yet the hardest thing to do.

It was only after my spiritual awakening that I understood what a therapist had been talking about all those years ago when working with me and Kenny. The therapist would pound on his chest and tell us to "speak from the heart." I had no idea what he meant. Now I get it—a heart that was open, that did not have the chaos and frustrations of modern life in the way; one that was okay being vulnerable and speaking truthfully from pure, unconditional love; not from a place of anger and resentment, not from a guarded heart.

I am forever grateful that I was able to experience this Nirvana so that I now know that there is a light at the end of the tunnel. I will continue to do my own healing work until I get there and as I do, I will guide others to do the same. Emerging from that place, then endeavoring to get better, that very journey has given me an entirely new view on my relationships, especially my role as a parent, a spouse, and a true friend.

Going through my own manic episode and spiritual awakening has given me a new view of mental health as well. When I was diagnosed with bipolar disorder, the first thing I thought to myself was YES, bipolar meaning two polarities; Heaven and Earth. I knew that something, let's call it "the Universe," was speaking to me! I was receiving messages from the TV and radio and when I shared this with my Rabbi, he said, "God speaks to people in different ways."

This helped me feel more at peace but it also confused me because for 48 years, I *never* believed in God or a Higher Power and now this "thing" was actively communicating with me? To this day, my hubby doesn't fully understand this. Thankfully, he has experienced some "out there" things which he can't explain, so he is open to trying to understand. It's this open mind and heart that kept him from running far, far away from me.

When I say the "Universe" this can mean loved ones that have passed away, angels, spirit guides, Ascended Masters, Guardian Angels, God and the list goes on. These are what we call 'of the Light.' However, there are also dark forces out there as well. I am not a fan of the term demons, but that is one term that can be used to describe the darkness. When we receive messages from the Light, they are soft, loving and peaceful messages. When we receive messages from the Dark, they are more aggressive, anxiety promoting and often negative.

For example, when someone hears a message that tells them to do something negative, it's of the Darkness. God and his messengers only come from unconditional love and would *never* tell someone to do something negative.

When I was diagnosed with bipolar disorder, one of my healers was a Chinese acupuncturist. She told me that Eastern philosophy believes that if a person is diagnosed with bipolar disorder at the age of thirteen years old or older, then they are holding onto a strong resentment (more like a toxic hatred) towards someone. If a child is diagnosed with bipolar disorder under the age of thirteen, then Eastern philosophy believes that one of the child's parents is holding onto this toxic resentment, and it's usually towards one of the grandparents. Therefore, it seems that bipolar disorder is more of a dis-ease of the heart, one that is strongly affecting the mind.

As we heal our hearts, our brain chemistry changes. This is how I was able to wean off my medications. Mind you, this was a long and painful process, but doable if we are willing to humble ourselves to work hard through the pain and resentment. Moving from the attitude of "life happens to me" to "life happens for me" is transformative! The sooner we can encourage movement toward healing these wounds, the better off our lives and health will be.

I believe those of us who have had bigger traumas in our lives first met our challenges even before we incarnated. Because of this there are healers among us to help transform our world. However, in the past, society has medicated them, locked them up and often thrown away the key. If I had my episode before 2014, I know this would have been me. The people around us would have insisted that I was bat-shit crazy claiming that God and angels were communicating with me. If Moses, Jesus, and Abraham were here today, can you imagine what they would have been diagnosed with? Would clinicians have considered bipolar disorder, schizophrenia, a psychotic break …?

As I always say, the bigger the gift, the bigger the challenge. Look at all of the famous people that have been diagnosed with bipolar disorder, then look at the great gifts they have shared with the world. Selena Gomez has been very open about her mental health challenges, for example. She struggled in her 20's before being diagnosed with bipolar disorder.

In an interview in *Rolling Stone*, Selena explained that she had "started to feel like I was not in control of what I was feeling, whether that was really great or really bad." Her disorder was causing dramatic shifts in her energy, as well as in her mood and thought processing.

"I've been to four treatment centers," Selena told *Rolling Stone*. She had suffered psychosis and suicidal ideation. She admitted to having thought that the world would be better if she wasn't in it. This is astonishing for her fans to hear—for them nothing could be further from the truth.

Selena Gomez continues to give us amazing work as a Grammy-nominated singer, movie actor, movie producer, and now as a television actor, brilliant in her role in *Only Murders in the Building*. Once she understood what was happening, and how to create balance in her life, she was able to continue in her brilliant career.

Healing was a lot of hard work, she admitted. She created a documentary with AppleTV+, *Selena Gomez: My Mind and Me*, to explain her mental health journey.

The incomparable Mariah Carey has also been open about facing her bipolar disorder. She told *People* magazine that for some time she resisted accepting that this was her challenge, that she lived in "denial and isolation and in constant fear someone would expose me."

Eventually she realized there was no reason to keep denying her reality. "It was too heavy a burden to carry and I simply couldn't do that anymore," she said. And when she stood in her truth, and found the healing she needed, she felt blessed. "I sought and received treatment," she told *People*. "I put positive people around me and I got back to doing what I love—writing songs and making music."

I don't mean to suggest that bipolar disorder—or any mental health disorder—is the terrain of artists and celebrities. Mental health disorders are not confined by boundaries. They appear all over the world, throughout history, in all genders, and across every socio-economic profile. It is believed that many people who contributed brilliantly to our lives suffered from bipolar disorder, including Steve Jobs, Alvin Ailey, Earnest Hemingway, Winston Churchill, Virginia Woolf, Vincent van Gogh, and Beethoven.

Sometimes our perspective can change even with a simple word choice. I have a client who recoils at the word *trauma*. I asked her to replace it with *drama*, just as an exercise. The goal was not to minimize her trauma of course, just to allow her to let go of a word that was causing her to panic. Once she could explain the details of her drama, instead of her trauma, she was able to speak more freely and we were able to get to work.

In recent years the concept of generational trauma (generational drama) has made its way into mainstream media discussions. This is fascinating to me—the realization that we carry with us the burdens and heartaches and hopefully also the joy of our ancestors—and something I continue to study. I am fascinated by reminders that the mind is porous. It can absorb new experiences and information. Even if there is a period where it is taking in too much which can feel overwhelming, it does in time become absorbent again. There is always renewal. And this porous mind makes for a rich spiritual, inner world.

I think it is worth investigating what our ancestors have sent forward, both the bad and the good. In reading Robert Falconer's tour-de-force, *The Others Within Us*, I came across a fascinating truth. It is a fairly modern stance that the mind is private property. Throughout history and across cultures, beliefs have existed about visitors to the mind, about the spirit of others traveling in and out of our being. While today's creators in the horror genre—in books, films, plays, and even video games—have made a great deal out of terrifying visits through stories of possession and exorcism, the vast majority of these visits are thought to be peaceful, gentle, intended to enlighten and even inspire.

We are not meant to be afraid of our minds. In fact, we are meant to be open to changes and to learn from the new experiences that occur there. What would happen if we were able to perceive more about our inner world? What if we become fully open to receiving gifts that might arrive there?

In my thinking, there is a fine line between schizophrenics and mediums. Mediums are able to communicate with those of the Light; people diagnosed with schizophrenia usually experience the Dark. What if we taught these people how to energetically protect themselves from the Dark and taught them how to use their gifts to communicate with the Light? I have had so many clients work with psychics and mediums to help them connect with and heal relationships with those that have passed away.

I too have had transformational experiences healing my relationship with both of my parents after they had passed away. Both of my parents had mental illnesses. It took my dad one and a half years to come through with a psychic/medium and tell me that he was sorry. Then, just the other day, I was told that he is having a hard time working on his own healing but that God was keeping him accountable for his actions. Wow! This blew my mind. I hope that I don't lose too many of you here while sharing this with you.

I have a few clients who have lost their children to cancer or had children who died by suicide. Referring them to some of my gifted Psychic/Mediums has transformed their lives! Yes, they are still in pain, that's true, but now they know that their children are always with them, and some have even learned how to communicate with them in meaningful ways.

Do you know anyone that has experienced a psychotic break (besides me, lol)? I believe that there is a fine line between psychosis and psychics. I was working with a client, Maggie, who was a born-again Christian. She shared with me that she had a psychotic break. I asked Maggie to tell me about it and immediately she shared with me that there was a man in her community who died by suicide. She had not known him when he was alive.

Maggie said that she had been aware of his tragic death, because the entire community was talking about it, and during her psychotic break he came to her like a close friend and told her what had happened before he jumped off of that cliff. He said that he stepped towards the edge, then stepped back. He had been interrupted momentarily by a thought that maybe he didn't need to die after all. It wasn't a confusing moment, it was a cleansing one.

He then heard a voice that told him to go ahead, that it was time, so he walked back to the end of the cliff and jumped. Later, when Maggie researched his death online, she found that it was just as he told her—there were witness reports that he had stepped aside for a moment, as if he wasn't going to jump, then did.

People around Maggie were aghast when she told them this story. They told Maggie such a vision was the work of the devil. As a result of sharing this vision, she was heavily medicated. I said to her, "what if this was a gift? It's possible you have a gift from God and this wasn't the devil's work at all." I wanted her to look at this in a new way, to not retreat in fear. I wanted her to agree, to imagine learning how to use this kind of gift to help herself, and even to assist others.

These days Maggie is heavily medicated and resigned to the idea that her vision was a dark force at work. This breaks my heart. She is suffering when quite possibly the light is there—and she can follow an alternate path to alleviate her suffering and connect with others. I know some of you are thinking this is idealistic of me, to believe this darkness is really a path to light, but I do believe it, and I pray for a peaceful future for Maggie.

This is one of the many areas where our HUGS healers can help those experiencing mental health challenges to remove the darkness, to push away the possibility of negative forces at work, and welcome a brighter future, to literally bring in the Light. I know this will sound abstract to some, but over the years it has become definitive to me that this is the work we need to do urgently.

So: let's get to work at changing the narrative from "crazy" to "crazy amazing!"

I have been speaking (well typing, lol) about several more severe mental health challenges. Let's talk also about the very familiar challenges of fear, anxiety, depression, and loneliness, that can feel every bit as severe as a diagnosed disease or disorder. The fact is, humans feel lonely.

Let's think about this for a moment. Who wouldn't feel lonely in a world where we left our Heavenly Mother and Divine Father and were born into a world where we don't know anyone? Our souls will always yearn to be with our spirituality and there will be an unavoidable emptiness because of it. Let's say that again. *Our souls will always yearn to be with our spiritual family and there will be an unavoidable emptiness because of it.* It has become essential to me to be mindful of this.

Without better solutions, many throughout history have tried to fill this emptiness by self-medicating with drugs, alcohol, and a wide array of various fixations. Such addictions can only move us further away from our spirituality, by numbing our instincts, by disrupting our perspective, by inhibiting our mindfulness and creativity and intellectual curiosity, by hiding us from our gifts.

What if we could address this emptiness before addictions enter our lives? What if we found or formed deeper connections to the Universe?

What if we can learn how to reconnect with our divine family and our own Divinity?

I believe now I was blessed to have a spiritual awakening. However, it was hard for me to arrive at the word *blessed* because I understood also this awakening had resulted from severe childhood trauma. There was a hurt inner child I needed to acknowledge. She needed more than my attention. She needed my love.

God had blessed me with three beautiful children that I knew immediately how to love with a deep-soul knowing that required no prompting or learning. I would go to the ends of the Earth for their peace, safety, and contentment. But I did need to learn how to nurture the hurt child inside of me. I needed to learn how to connect with her in my heart, and reparent her the way I would have wanted to be parented. I always say that I was given the parents I needed, not the ones I wanted.

One evening, I had been through an out-of-body experience where my soul was one with the White Light. This was an incredible feeling and a hard one to explain, but today I can mentally go back there, thanks to my meditation practice. This allows me to experience and explore that state of bliss I experienced on that special night. And with the way things are going in our society today, we all can use a mental and emotional escape.

Have you ever heard of the saying "When we pray, we speak to God; when we meditate, we hear from God?" When we can quiet our monkey brains and all of the noise, we can hear our inner voice. Many refer to this as the voice of God.

I attended an event at UCLA in the summer of 2024. Oprah Winfrey was interviewing the United States Surgeon General, Dr. Vivek Murthy. Without hesitation he said that one out of every two Americans are experiencing significant loneliness and it's going to take a spiritual awakening to change this. I am on a mission to do just that. But it's not an easy process. It requires us to let down our guard, reconnect with our inner child, and release what is keeping us from connecting to our true selves.

I spoke about empaths in Chapter Two: The Art of Sensitivity. We label children as having anxiety instead of noting that they are sensitive empaths, often feeling emotions in a way that prevents them from realizing these emotions are not originally their own.

There are so many of us that have unexplained fear. For example, I have a friend who is deathly afraid of dogs though she never had a negative experience with one. When working with a hypnotherapist, she realized that in a past life she was bitten quite savagely by a large, unrestrained dog. Her subconscious mind retained this fear from that lifetime into this one. She gave the hypnotherapist permission to release the memory. To overcome a fear, we must educate ourselves about it; we must understand its origin.

When news of the COVID-19 virus first came around there were many people who were deeply afraid, even before it was confirmed how catastrophic the pandemic would be. A few of my hypnotherapists said that they had worked with clients experiencing this fear intensely. What these clients had in common is that in a past life they had died in pandemic situations, from a virus or plague. In the course of one session, practitioners were able to work with these clients to release their fears. In many cases this kind of work meant clients were able to feel more secure and live more peacefully during the COVID-19 lockdowns.

I hope that with this example, and others, I have helped to open your eyes to alternative perspectives of mental health challenges, understanding that those with challenges also have gifts. The greater the gift, the greater the challenge. It's going to take all of us coming together to help make the shift to a healthier, less lonely, more vibrant and accepting world.

I invite you to join me in this life-changing movement.

THE PERSPECTIVE EXERCISES

Many spiritual teachings, including *A Course in Miracles*, remind us that we are the ones who assign meaning to everything in life. Nothing has inherent meaning on its own— we give it meaning based on our perceptions. This becomes clear when two people experience the same event in completely different ways. One person might see a dog walking by and feel warmth and joy, while another might feel anxious or afraid. These differences arise because, most of the time, we are not experiencing reality as it truly is. Instead, we are filtering it through the lens of our past experiences, cultural conditioning, and deeply held beliefs.

Often, it's not the situation itself that causes us suffering, but the story we attach to it. Since we are the ones assigning meaning, then we also have the power to shift our perspective. This shift is crucial because the way we perceive an experience shapes how we respond to it—and ultimately, the outcomes we create in our lives.

This exercise is designed to help you release limiting, negative thought patterns and adopt a more flexible, positive perspective. In doing so, you'll cultivate greater peace and joy, allowing you to navigate any situation in a way that leads to growth, connection, and the best possible outcomes.

If writing isn't your preference, simply take a moment to self-reflect and visualize your answers.

Activity: The Shifting Your Perspective Journal

Step One: Identify the trigger. What was the moment that stung?

Close your eyes. Take a deep breath. Think of a recent moment that triggered negative emotions for you. Write it down in one sentence.

Example: "My friend didn't respond to my message, and I feel invisible."

Step Two: Uncover the hidden belief. What are you telling yourself?

What thought immediately arises in response to this situation? What are you believing about yourself, the other person, or the world? *Example:* "I believe I am not important to others."

Step Three: Ask the four sacred questions.

This step is inspired by "The Work," a platform by Byron Katie, author of *Loving What Is, A Thousand Names for Joy,* and *A Mind at Home with Itself.*

Take this uncovered belief and examine it like a compassionate detective, using these four questions:

1. Is it true? (Be honest. Simply yes or no.)

2. Can you absolutely, 100% know that it's true? (Pause. What if there's more to the story?)

3. How do you react—emotionally, physically, mentally—when you believe this thought? (Describe the sensations in your body, the emotions that arise, the behaviors that follow.)

4. Who would you be without this thought? (Feel into this version of yourself. Are you lighter? Freer? More open?)

Step Four: This is the turnaround. Find your new, expansive truth.

Let's rewrite the story. Find at least three ways this belief could be untrue or have a different meaning.

- Turnaround One: "I *am* important to others." (Think of moments when you have felt important to others.)

- Turnaround Two: "Others are not important to me." (Think of moments when you were able to stay connected to what is true for you despite other's opinions or behaviors.)

- Turnaround Three: "I'm important to myself." (Think of what happens, how your body responds when you give yourself the attention and validation you need.)

Step Five: Embody the shift. Embrace a new perspective.

Take a deep breath. Notice how you feel and behave when you connect to the more empowering and positive perspective. How do you feel about the situation? Do you feel lighter? Less constricted? More open?

Let this practice be a gateway to seeing beyond assumptions and into the deeper truths of love and connection.

6

THE ART OF REFLECTION

(see also: impression, meditation, observation)

When a glass reflects light, it lets us see things in a new way. When we think reflectively, we are able to mine new ideas, to see connections that we hadn't noticed before, and to change direction if we need to. Reflection allows us to strengthen and improve our critical thinking skills. In reflective thinking, we guide ourselves away from assumptions, away from taking things for granted. We see clearer paths to gratitude.

Whenever a parent shares with me details of their child's behaviors, how they annoy or bother them, the first question I always ask is *why?* "What about their behavior pushes your buttons?" The answers always seem to come from an egocentric place of embarrassment, guilt, shame, hurt, or lack of control, and the list goes on.

Using this strategy and analyzing my most challenging years in raising Jordan, I had many *ah-ha* moments. For example, as a child I always felt different from others. Having two parents with severe mental health challenges and not being able to speak to anyone about this made me feel all alone and different from others. Then, when my son was diagnosed with Asperger's and ADHD, I again faced the emotional turmoil of feeling "different" from others. Pain from my past circled the pain in my present, even if I wasn't fully aware of the emotions that were resurfacing.

I was certain that other moms had no idea what I was going through as I observed them with their "perfect" children. Again, I felt all alone, that I wasn't able to share this with anyone. I felt different from the other parents, sure they would never understand my family or me.

Realizing now that children mirror issues that their parents get to (or *need to*) heal— this has been incredibly eye-opening. We all have deep issues that need healing and our children reflect to us our own *misghigos*. As adults, we get to choose whether we want to look into the mirror and see what emotions our children are bringing up in us. With such a foundation, we might be able to better focus our attention on what our children are going through; we might become more equipped to help them.

I promise you, the best gift you can give to yourself, your family, and your child is to look inward and work on yourself as you simultaneously find resources to help your child. A good friend has a son who was diagnosed with severe autism. He is now in high school, playing varsity baseball. A combination of Western medicine and holistic healing was able to transform his behavior and welcome his remarkable progress. But there was more than that. This happened also because his mom had the courage to look in the mirror and do her own healing.

For me, raising a child with anxiety, ADHD, and Asperger's (which has been reclassified as spectrum disorder), had started off like a nightmare. I liked to be "in control" but my son was unpredictable. It was usually the unpredictability that threw me into a tizzy. After parenting classes, plus private parenting therapy sessions together with Kenny, I learned to pick my battles (well, most of the time!). But during these therapy sessions no one ever asked me why Jordan's behaviors affected me so much. Why did my buttons keep getting pushed by his behaviors?

Recently, Kenny was reminding me how Jordan "taught us patience and compassion and the importance of checking our egos at the door." Wow! We used to think that raising a child on the spectrum was a curse. In hindsight, we both realize that it was a gift to help teach us what needed to be changed in *us*, not him, in order to live happier and healthier lives. This philosophy is profound. Instead of thinking about how this happened to us, we were thinking how this happened *for us*. It allowed us to grow, learn, and become better individuals, parents, and spouses.

It's amazing when we take a moment to sit back and reflect on our lives; as children, as adults, and as parents. I asked Kenny to share with us what it was like going through my manic episode/spiritual awakening as a spouse and a medical professional. He shared this with me and with his generosity and permission, I am sharing it with you:

When I was in medical school, I spent 2 months doing a psychiatric rotation at a VA Hospital. This was a requirement. I had no interest in psychiatry and honestly never even thought about mental health disorders before medical school or especially during the first 2 years of school. Sure, I learned about the disorders, neurological pathways, possible causes and pharmacologic treatments but I thought of it as a fiction novel not real disorders that happen to real people.

My rotation was during a frigid winter at the VA Hospital in Chicago. We were introduced to the in-patient ward staff, instructed on areas to go to and avoid and then assigned our patients to follow. I remember sitting in my first interview with an inpatient. When I arrived at the physician's consultation room the patient was already there sitting opposite the doctor. The patient had schizophrenia and was heavily medicated. He seemed harmless, cooperative and sedated. The session lasted 30 minutes with lots of questions about his medical progress, relationship with other patients, satisfaction with his accommodations and goals to accomplish.

When we were done, I stood up to say goodbye and open the door for him. When he stood up, I realized he was over 6 feet 10 inches tall and towered over me like a giant. I immediately went into fight or flight mode. I started sweating, was anxious, nervous, fearful and terrified all at the same time. I felt threatened that he was going to lash out at me. There was no basis for this fear. This was a fantasy I immediately fabricated in my mind from watching too many horror movies in the 70's. He politely grunted goodbye and was escorted back to the common area by a hospital orderly. It was at this exact moment when I realized I would either fear these patients or learn compassion. I chose fear.

As the rotation continued, I would study diseases and treatments. I knew the name of all the diseases, symptoms, possible causes and treatment options; I just couldn't put a face to each disorder because I was afraid of being with people who were psychologically different, diseased or afflicted. Bipolar, schizophrenia, multiple personality disorders and PTSD were cool to talk about and learn the medications that control the symptoms, but to see a person express these disorders live frightened me. Therefore, I avoided patient care for the remainder of my rotation. Sad, but true.

In May of 2014 my wife of 22 years experienced a manic episode. Looking back, I should have seen it coming like a dark rain cloud before the storm, but mostly I just accepted her growing bizarre behavior as eccentric. She always had a type A, outgoing and friendly personality. She has always had a lot of friends, been extremely cordial to everyone and made everyone feel loved. They wanted to be in her presence. As her mania slowly progressed to a head, I noticed that many of her friends were not around. Maybe they were growing weary of her changing personality and possibly frightened by her overly talkative and unusual behavior and mannerisms. She became obsessed with objects, people, and certain situations bordering on psychiatric and then BAM!

I was away the weekend of May 23, 2014 at a retreat in Colorado. It was one of the few times I went away without my wife. The first night I was gone she reached the pinnacle of her disease and by the next day I was on a plane home. By 8:00 that night we were embraced. I didn't want to let her go because I would then have to make some very difficult decisions. With the help of a dear friend who is a psychologist, we decided that seeing a psychologist and a psychiatrist the next day we would hopefully be able to keep her from being admitted to an inpatient setting. Luckily with the help of her providers she was started on medication and began her healing journey.

Over the next six months she underwent her own type of transformation. As she proclaims: 'I went from medication to meditation'. She finished a short course of three heavy medications and a lot of therapy and then started an intensive alternative treatment plan. Between hypnotherapy, energy healing, shamans, yoga, meditation and religious counseling she was transformed. She wasn't back, she was better than ever!

I have never been so frightened, anxious, fearful or sad during those first few days of her diagnosis. Medical diseases affect your physical health, mental disorders change your personality. Was she going to be the same woman I fell in love with 35 years ago? Was she going to be someone I admire or someone I dislike? Cancer, heart disease and diabetes weaken you physically but diet, exercise and medication can improve your health. Mental disease changes your personality and even with intensive healing you are never the same as before. Many are eternally sedated, some are emotionally blunted and some are enlightened. Hopefully most are the latter which enables them to thrive. With wisdom comes growth and prosperity.

I love my wife now more than ever. Not because of all the good that she has done over the last ten years but because she has evolved into an even more amazing person who has empathy, sympathy and love for people and healing.

My wife took her experience and decided to help others. She started a mental health awareness foundation called the Extraordinary Lives Foundation (ELF) in 2015. This started as a foundation to help bring awareness to mental health issues concentrating on pediatric and adolescent youth. Her belief is that mental health issues begin in early childhood and worsen over time if not recognized and treated. What starts out as a behavioral issue can spiral into mental and emotional challenges. Mara and ELF host several awareness events in the community and around the country.

Mara then started the HUGS Healing Center, which she refers to as her life mission: The HUGS Healing Center offers a directory of Practitioners that offer an array of alternative healing options and educational resources to complement the treatment of mental health challenges. They provide an intuitive discovery call which can be transformative. Their goal is to bridge the gap between Western medicine and holistic healing, offering an integrative approach to emotional wellness for the entire family. I refer several of my patient's to HUGS and the results have been phenomenal.

On a more personal note, my wife decided to address my own medical issue: anxiety. I had a significant and handcuffing fear of being late. Late to the airport, dinner with friends, or getting to the office on time. Worst part is I started imprinting this emotion onto my children. My excuse for ignoring this disease was my ignorance in how it is affecting my life. Finally, I agreed to see an alternative healer and in 45 minutes I was healed. Hypnotherapy allowed me to identify my past trauma and release it from my subconscious. Sounds unbelievable but over the last eight years I have confirmed my remission in multiple examples and feel amazing.

As you can tell this is a very personal and important topic to me. I discuss and offer help to all my patients by encouraging an open dialog. I then recommend therapy with psychologists, psychiatrists, hypno-therapists, alternative healers, clergy: anyone or any approach that they choose.

I am so grateful that Kenny was there to support me and never considered running away when the going got tough. Mental health and emotional challenges have significant effects on the entire family. We get to choose if we want to let these junctures break us or make us better and stronger than ever. I pray that you choose the second option for your loved ones and I promise you will not regret it.

THE REFLECTION EXERCISES

Over the past few decades, science has deepened our understanding of mirror neurons, revealing the profound connection between parents and their children. This bond is especially evident in early childhood, where children naturally reflect their parents' emotions, behaviors, and subconscious patterns. While this mirroring can sometimes be challenging and even frustrating, it also presents one of the greatest opportunities for healing and growth.

Children act as mirrors, revealing not only our strengths but also the parts of ourselves we may ignore or suppress. Through their behavior, they unknowingly highlight what within us needs the most attention and healing.

This exercise will guide you through a process of self-reflection and awareness, helping you uncover the hidden gifts within your children's challenging behaviors. Embracing this journey of healing is not only transformative for you—it is also one of the most valuable gifts you can give your child.

Exercise One: EFT Tapping Exercise: From Trigger to Transformation

Gary Craig created Emotional Freedom Technique (EFT), also known as "tapping", in the 1990s. Craig is a Stanford-educated engineer who is also a certified master practitioner of Neuro-linguistic programming. The purpose of this technique is to help parents shift from frustration to a sense of ease, using their child's behavior as a mirror for personal growth.

A video guide for this technique is available at marajjames.com.

Step One: Identify the trigger.

Think of a situation where your child's behavior triggered a strong emotional reaction in you.

Write down the answers to these questions:

- What exactly did they say or do, what was their behavior? [This will be the behavior that we will use in step three.]

- What emotions did you feel (e.g., anger, frustration, sadness, helplessness)? [This will be the emotion that we will use in step three.]

- What belief about yourself is underneath your emotional reaction to their behavior (e.g., "I'm not respected," "I'm failing as a parent," "I'm not in control")? [This will be the limiting belief that we will use in step three.]

Step Two: Rate the intensity.

How intense is your emotional reaction to this trigger on a scale from zero to ten?

Step Three: Create your set-up statement.

Tap on the karate chop point (the side of your hand) and repeat the following statement three times using the *behavior, emotion and limiting belief* from step one.

"Even though I feel [emotion] when my child does [behavior], and it brings up [limiting belief], I deeply love and accept myself."

Example: *"Even though I feel disrespected when my child talks back to me, and it makes me believe I'm failing as a parent, I deeply love and accept myself."*

Step Four: Use this tapping sequence.

Repeat each phrase after me, while tapping the corresponding points:

1. **Eyebrows:** *I acknowledge this frustration with my child with kindness.*

2. **Side of Eyes:** *I feel so triggered by this and I am willing to explore this deeper.*

3. **Under Eyes:** *It makes me feel frustrated and I can respond with awareness*

4. **Under Nose:** *I don't like feeling this way. I choose to see my child as a teacher.*

5. **Chin:** *What if this is showing me something deeper and I can release this old pattern?*

6. **Collarbones:** *What if this is an invitation to heal? I choose to heal, and my child heals with me.*

7. **Under Arms:** *Maybe my child is mirroring something in me. I am growing, learning, and evolving.*

8. **Top of Head:** *I am open to seeing this differently. I embrace this challenge as an opportunity for healing.*

Step Five: Reassess the intensity.

Take a deep breath. Check in with yourself—has the intensity of your emotions changed compared to the intensity you noticed on step two? What is the intensity now? If new insight came up for you, tap on that emotion. If no new insight came up for you and the intensity is higher than a three, repeat the process with a focus on self-compassion and releasing resistance. Keep repeating the process until you reach a three or lower.

Step Six: Remember integration and affirmation.

Close with this affirmation:

"I am becoming more aware, more present, and more compassionate with myself and my child. Every challenge is an opportunity for growth."

Note: EFT practitioners may approach this process in different ways, but all methods are effective.

Exercise Two: Healing Processes and Practices

Here are some practices to help you use self-reflection for healing and growth.

A. Practice self-awareness and mindfulness.

When a trigger arises, practice deep breathing and pause before reacting. Acknowledge your emotional response, and identify the underlying need or fear that is being activated. This awareness helps you separate your own emotions from your child's behavior.

B. Journal to use triggers as an invitation for growth.

Reframe triggers as opportunities for growth. When you're triggered, ask yourself, "What is this experience teaching me about myself?" This shift in perspective can help you take responsibility for your emotional reactions while also deepening your self-awareness.

C. Seek inner child healing.

Engage in practices that nurture and heal your inner child. This might involve re-parenting your inner child by speaking kindly to yourself, practicing self-compassion, or visualizing moments of safety, love, and care that you didn't receive as a child.

D. Set boundaries with compassion.

It's important for you to learn healthy boundaries with your children. Setting limits with love and respect (rather than from a place of anger or fear) allows both you and your child to feel safe and respected.

E. Look to parenting groups and therapeutic support.

Joining a parenting support group can provide a safe space for you to share your experiences, reflect on your triggers, and receive feedback from others who are also working through similar issues. Working with a therapist or holistic practitioner, especially one who specializes in healing trauma, can help you uncover the deep-rooted emotional issues you may be carrying. Healing therapies can provide tools to manage triggers and heal from past wounds.

F. Apply mindful communication.

Practice compassionate communication or other mindful communication techniques that promote empathy and understanding. This can help you express your needs and feelings in a way that is more constructive and less reactive.

G. Engage in self-compassion.

Parents often experience guilt or shame when they recognize that their reactions are connected to their past. It's important to practice self-compassion, acknowledging that *everyone* has triggers, and that healing is a process. Offer yourself the same kindness you would offer a friend in similar circumstances.

By engaging in these reflective processes, you can begin to uncover the deeper emotional currents that shape your parenting. Understanding these patterns allows for more conscious, compassionate responses to both you and your child.

7

THE ART OF HEALING

(see also: restoring, mending, invigorating)

*H*ealing begins the very moment we commit to making inner peace a priority. When we choose healing, we are often attaining spirituality and reclaiming our lives.

Pain is inevitable in our lives but healing *is* possible! My heart knows this to be true. It takes us stepping out of our comfort zone, moving the ego aside, and mustering up courage to begin our personal healing journey.

It's probably no surprise that healing has become one of my favorite topics. My goal is to inspire, educate and guide others along their healing journeys. I can easily imagine writing an entire book on this topic (possibly my next book!).

Most references define healing as the process of making or becoming sound or healthy again. When I was growing up, this word was only used when someone was healing from a physical ailment, and there was no question that this kind of healing was essential. Who knew that there were ways to heal our emotions, or that we even needed to do this in order to live a truly happy life? Surely not me!

It wasn't until I experienced my manic episode that I learned that healing was going to be at the center of my life. At first, I thought that I wanted to heal so that I could get back to my old way of living and it was the only chance I had if I was going to be able to be weaned off of all of my medication. Let me start by saying that I *never* want to go back to my old way of living.

I now realize that I always had undiagnosed PTSD. I was constantly in a state of flight or fight. Not knowing about my childhood trauma until I was 52 years old was a blessing but also a curse because it kept me in a state of constant anxiety, one of the worst things for our physical, mental and emotional well-being.

Before I was able to truly begin my healing journey, I needed to be medically stabilized. I worked with a psychiatrist and a therapist and once I was stable, the Universe began introducing me to a variety of holistic healers, each with unique healing modalities.

The therapist that I was initially working with was very spiritual but he kept saying to me "we almost lost you."

I bit my tongue because I wanted to tell him that we didn't almost lose me. I was supposed to experience all of this so I could have first-hand knowledge of what a spiritual awakening was truly about; how it can be misdiagnosed as a mental health challenge (bipolar disorder, schizophrenia, or a psychotic break); and how it can become a gift.

It has been said that everything in our external world reflects our inner world. When I think back to raising my children, to my friendships and family members, I realize that there is truth to this statement. One of my goals during my healing journey was to become un-perturb-able so that no matter what anyone said or did to me, I would not allow it to negatively affect me. Trust me, this has been an ongoing challenge for me. After years (and years and years) of intense healing, meditating, and creating a gratitude practice, I am happy to say that I am closer to this goal now more than ever.

The Universe is on a constant mission for us to grow and heal, so it challenges us by sending us people that will push our buttons, including our children. I received a message from the Universe once saying "We are all on a journey to heal, but we are ignoring our mission." I told God, "Thank you for the message, I will make sure to share it with the world." I continue to think about this and use life's challenges as opportunities to grow and amplify my learning. There is always more good work to do and the journey to freedom is well worth it!

I encourage everyone experiencing challenges to be open to looking at their root causes. I have seen over and over again that the Universe will keep sending us situations similar to our childhood traumas until we heal from those initial experiences and circumstances. For example, I was working with a client whose mother was a narcissist. My client ended up marrying (and divorcing) a narcissist. She didn't realize it, but she kept dating narcissists until I pointed this out to her. She agreed to begin working on releasing the resentment she held onto towards her mother. Her hard work paid off and she is now engaged to a wonderful man who is healthy, peaceful, and not a narcissist. I have seen this over and over again. When we release our childhood trauma and drama, we don't manifest similar situations anymore in our present life. We can end the pain and move forward into our more peaceful lives.

Healing begins with us being willing to put our pinky toe into the water. There is no need to jump in all the way on the first day. Baby steps is all it takes. We just have to be willing to do the work. More specifically, we need to stop turning away from our discomfort.

We need to lean toward our discomfort and ask, *what can I learn from this?* One of the greatest gifts that we can give to ourselves is to move from "life happens to me" and towards "life happens for me." This can be a VERY challenging task to accomplish but trust me, it's a journey worth taking.

I attended a day of healing at the Kabbalah Center in Los Angeles with a dear friend of mine. Kabbalah scholars taught us that the third part of the saying "Life happens to us, life happens for us" is "life then happens through us." Wow!

Once we have worked on healing and clearing ourselves, we are able to allow the Universe to work through us so that we can help others. And trust me, this is a magical experience. I used to live with so much fear and resentment. I now live in a more blissful and joyful state. We all can move on from fear, anger, sadness, shame, blame, and guilt toward peace, faith, love, and trust. We just need to be open to taking the first steps.

Recently I spoke with a gentleman who was diagnosed with bipolar disorder. He felt that he was doing well while taking five mental health medications. His life used to be "a hot mess," as he would say, and now, he is happily married and stable.

I wondered—but was not yet ready to ask him—if he worked on healing his heart by releasing any resentments that he was holding onto. Would this question be helpful to him? Maybe not. As long as each of us are happy and living peaceful lives, that is all that matters.

Several months later, I saw a Facebook post by this same gentleman. He had posted a video, sharing challenges he was facing. Though he was still taking five medications he was experiencing a deep state of depression. I wanted to reach out to him to offer my support, but knew he was not in a place to receive it. He had chosen to stay firmly in a state of "life happens to me" and was not willing to embrace a healing journey. Perhaps that's meant to be—it's not for me to say. There is always his next life where he can choose to embrace the journey.

In order for us to live a truly happy and peaceful life, it is important to release our complications—those negative energies that disrupt our potential and prevent us from living more peaceful lives. Many of us hold onto negative emotions to the point that they eat us up inside, even in the moments we are not consciously aware of them. God loves us unconditionally (thus the title of this book) but we don't unconditionally love ourselves or others. What if we could learn to do this? To treat ourselves with this level of love and grace?

Many of us were hurt by a parent or by another trusted adult as we were growing up. It is important to remember that in many instances "hurt people hurt people" or "traumatized people traumatize people." I do not say this to free them of accountability and I certainly do not say this to trivialize your painful past experiences in any way. Likewise, I do not think the burden of forgiveness, too often manipulated, needs to fall on the hurt person.

Letting go of negativity can be different from forgiveness—you will know the balance that works for you. More than anything, I want us to understand that letting go of negative emotions toward the person that hurt you is transformative.

Conversely, when we continue to live with the weight of negativity, we are living in a way that allows that heavy toxicity too much power. I think of it like this: the poison that might have killed them is threatening to kill us instead. Let's put an end to that now. Let's soothe and heal our hurt inner child and give ourselves the more peaceful future that every human deserves.

Let me say more on how this works. In *The Myth of the Normal*, Dr. Gabor Mate defines the way in which all children have a deep inner need to feel safe. Children have a non-negotiable need to feel secure. When a child has been abused, instead of hanging onto anger and fear and negativity about the abuse, instead of rejecting the abusive parent, the child might cling to them. But what happened to the anger, fear, and negativity? It had to go somewhere.

Most often, abused children turn those negative emotions towards themselves to save themselves from turning it toward the parent. They multiply their own trauma by internalizing their parent's negative behaviors. They direct the anger, shame, even disgust, toward themselves. This is a hard pill to swallow. It may take years, decades, before someone who was abused as a child is able to articulate what happened to them and receive trauma-informed care.

For me, I wasn't even aware of my childhood trauma until I was 52 years old and had been doing intensive therapy and healing for four years. It is amazing how protective our subconscious minds can be, but in the long run, these negative experiences end up turning into emotional or physical dis-eases.

Dr. Mate explains that trauma is an invisible force that shapes the way we live, the way we love, and the way we make sense of the world. It's at the root of our deepest wounds, but if we actively heal those wounds, we can reshape our lives. I ask you to have the courage to look at your past, as I did, because it's worth the journey to forgive one's self, as well as others.

Uh oh, I said the "F" word! I know that the very notion of forgiveness can be triggering to many of us. Trust me, I swore that I would never forgive my father! But as the years went on, I realized that if I wanted to be weaned off of all of my medication and transform my broken heart and my mental state of being, I was going to have to do the work. You will notice that often I will use the word "release" instead of "forgive." This word seems to be less triggering and the last thing we want to do to ourselves or others is to trigger them.

Again, it is important to understand that forgiveness/releasing does not mean that what the other person did is okay. It just means freedom for us, and aren't we worth it? I never have had to tell my father that I forgave him, but it was necessary for me to release the toxic emotions I was holding onto. In letting that go, my life has transformed beyond my wildest dreams.

Reparenting the child within you while you are also parenting the child or children in front of you is not for the faint of heart. It is the most trying and least acknowledged demand of parenthood. It is a marathon, not a sprint. Many of our parents and grand-parents believed they had to be tough with children because the world is tough. I think my generation and my kids' generation is proving this to be deeply flawed. You don't meet hard things with hardness. You conquer hard things with love.

For a while now, I've been saying that if you only remember one thing it should be to show your kids love. Because that's what they need. Thankfully I'm not alone in saying this. There are resounding cries from every corner of the world that we should rethink childcare practices from previous generations.

One key issue was that a parent's toughness too often made us afraid of them. As Dr. Tina Payne Bryson points out in her book *The Whole-Brained Child*, "We should never make our children afraid. They have a biological instinct that prompts them to go to a parent if they are afraid, and if that parent is the source of fear, it's confusing and creates a lot of stress in their nervous system."

When we teach our children to express emotions—all emotions, no matter how inconvenient they might be—we allow them to become adults who won't shut down the moment they feel anything other than happy. We don't have to be tough to teach resilience, we only have to be open and accepting, and that softness is so much easier than being hard, so let's embrace it. It is so important to love our kids a little extra on their bad days. Your child is not giving you a hard time, your child is having a hard time.

Childhood is not a race. Let's say that again. *Childhood is not a race.* There is no discernable reason we need to push our children to be the first to read, to write, to count, to score a goal or win a medal. There is a window of time for each child to develop at precisely the pace that is right for them. Think about your inner child as well. As a child, were you rushed into your own successes? Were you allowed to do things at your own pace? Do you treat your own inner child with patience and understanding?

This world needs all types of children. In the words of Angela Pruess, founder of Parents with Confidence, we need "the quiet, easy-going peacekeepers that sit still and observe; the loud shake-it-up, feel-it-deep changemakers that are always on the go, and every unique soul in between. Let's stop sending the message that only one type of child is a good child."

Kerwin Rae, a motivational speaker and high-performance specialist in Australia, has this reminder for us: "Our goal as parents is to build trust through conversation, not to build control through domination." The true measure of a mindful parent is an ability to meet your children where they are. More often than not, a child treated with respect will not have to spend their adult years trying to learn that they are worthy of it. And trust me, this process is grueling.

It is amazing what can happen when considering new vantage points, when we adjust that personal kaleidoscope we carry throughout the day. At a recent event hosted by the Extraordinary Lives Foundation, a group of moms were talking about holiday gifts for their children. One mom, Jennifer, was explaining that she was thinking of a gift for her son who has ADHD and loves the game UNO. It's a classic card game where the cards have vibrant colors and symbols. Children play several hands to reach a score of five hundred. Jennifer's son already had six UNO sets, some vintage as the card designs had changed over the years. He liked all of them.

Other moms in the group immediately started naming game sets that included numbers and counting. Hannah, who had been quiet for most of the conversation, said that giving her own son a different game from the one he was fixated on might be upsetting to him, as if she was trying to deter him from the game he really loved. No matter what she said as she presented the gift, his interpretation might be that she had disapproved of *his* game choice. When he chose something, he was all-in. It sounded like maybe this was true of Jennifer's child as well.

Precision was important to Hannah's son; he was strict about these things and would want to stay with the game he had chosen. Hannah suggested to Jennifer finding an UNO game in Spanish or French, so that she was celebrating the game her son loved. The game would be the same, but still she was expanding his play. I loved this suggestion. The nuance of it seemed important—meaning that for many children, an adjustment is welcome where a change may not be. And observing this is part of trying to share in their view of the world, in meeting them where they are. Seeing our children at play and the rules they create for themselves can be both informative and transformative. It's also meaningful to think back to your own childhood. What games and types of play did you love and why?

I want to remind you that I did NOT choose to go on a healing journey. It was my spiritual awakening/manic episode that kick started it. For those of you who have no intention of healing your own lives, I 1000% understand because I was you! However, being on the other side of it, I want to strongly encourage you and your loved ones to embrace the journey so that you too can shift your lives from a state of fear, separation, anxiety and loneliness, to a place of peace, faith, love and trust. Truly heaven on Earth. It IS possible! We are not healing to be able to handle trauma. We are healing to be able to find joy.

As adults, many of us have accumulated layers of armor that prevent us from experiencing true happiness. When we have not healed our hurt inner child, there are parts of us that are closed off from the world, kept in isolation. Life healing happens when we pull the layers back and face the difficult truth that's reluctant to come out of hiding. It's hard work, but it will always be worth the effort.

Here is something I wish I had been told ages ago: healing isn't just something we need to do when we're hurting. It is the intentional act of preparing our lives for future harmony, peace and true happiness. Reiki master and wellness coach Nyle Beck says it well: "You have every right to change your mind, your opinions, your preferences, your beliefs, how you relate to others, who you hang out with, how you speak, how you behave, and how you go about living your life. Humans are designed to shift and grow. We expand our awareness and we heighten who we are."

At various times in our lives we hear directives like "control your emotions." And too many times we've interpreted that to mean avoid your emotions. Let's agree that avoidance ends today.

I saw a meme this morning that said "Feel your shit. Understand your shit. Just don't lose your shit." Okay, but if we do lose our shit, let's find our way back. Let's embrace a new day.

Lately I've been reflecting on the early days of Jordan's diagnoses. Kenny and I had been the first of our friends to have children. Even with our strong ties to the medical community, it took us some time and effort to line up the support systems that Jordan needed, that we all needed.

And then, even when things got better, there would be this odd sort of scrutiny from certain members of the parenting community. They weren't necessarily conscious of their scrutiny; they just couldn't help themselves. A mom friend might say, "He seems to be doing great lately. Does he really need all those supports?" And I'd have to explain that he was thriving because he was appropriately supported.

As I learned more about neurodivergence I realized how many of us it affects. Recently I had a great conversation with a client who suffers from anxiety in her work place. I asked her how her coworkers could better support her. She said she wishes they understood that it can be hard for her to move between tasks with little notice. She said that she has a hard time when people schedule meetings with her without stating what the meeting will cover. It made her sick with worry. She had a similar concern about mass emails. If there was a group email about an issue with the team, or the work was falling short in some way, she would assume she was the problem.

That her initial assumptions turned out to be false mattered little because she had suffered in the time between the email and the resolution. "If there's a problem with my work, they should address me directly," she said. "That sounds reasonable," I assured her.

She said that due to her neurodivergence, co-workers were hesitant with assigning deadlines. They would say "no rush" or "whenever you can get to it" thinking this would calm her. "Give me deadlines, please," she implored them. She needed the structure.

Telling her "no rush" might mean it would never get done. "That's understandable," I told her.

Attention for the needs of others can be profound.

Recently, we were asked by HOAG Hospital in Newport Beach, California, to host a training for their therapists whose patients were hearing and seeing things that others were not. We called the workshop "Understanding Subtle Senses." The training was well received and one therapist said that she had a patient who was actively seeing spirits. The patient's mother and grandmother had scared her, telling her that those visions were the devil's work. This put the patient in tremendous fear.

Imagine when this patient considered that she might actually have a gift from God; when she considered that she could embrace these messages instead of fearing or running away from them? If Moses, Jesus, or Abraham were alive today, what would they have been diagnosed with when they claimed that they spoke to God?

When I had my spiritual awakening, I intrinsically knew that my journey was to break the cycle of how we treat mental health challenges. I began seeing a hypnotherapist who was able to speak to me on my level of understanding. He appreciated what I was experiencing when I shared about hearing and seeing "things." I will always be grateful for my psychiatrist and therapist for stabilizing me and keeping me from being locked up like they used to do not too long ago. But it was my team of holistic healers that helped me do the deep, transformative work. They helped me heal, to wean off of my medication, and to transform my life.

Maybe the things we thought we knew—or the things our elders thought they knew—don't apply to your own unique experience on Earth. Maybe we need to give ourselves the gift of opening our minds to new possibilities.

My friend and colleague, Aimee, a life coach and healer, confided in me that she continually questions whether mental illness is what we think it is, whether it is illness at all. Before I continue, I want to warn you that I understand that this might sound crazy, so please read this with an open mind. *What if this thing we call mental illness is just an extreme sensitivity to the things we cannot see?*

What if, indeed. Aimee shared with me that her client, Andrew, can see into other dimensions. He can interact with other beings. And as time goes on, Aimee no longer believes these are simply Andrew's hallucinations. This is not a boy who is impaired, she told me, this is a child living at a different frequency than you and I are living at right now. Maybe we are deeply flawed in our assertions that this is an illness.

I like that Aimee has pulled back her vantage point to allow for this possibility.

Be gentle with yourself. Healing is not about timelines and expectations—it's about being open to new thinking. Remember, it is a marathon, never a sprint. It's about moving pieces gently into their rightful places, not about forcing them to fit. Try giving yourself the space to allow your heart to find its peace. Your growth may be uncomfortable at times, but trust me, it's worth it. And it is the best gift that you can give to you and your family! There is no growth in the comfort zone, and no comfort in the growth zone.

I was working with a 21-year-old, Tessa, who was concerned that she was showing signs of borderline personality disorder (BPD). I was proud of Tessa for the self-awareness she was showing in talking to me. BPD is said to be the most serious in young adulthood.

It's a fairly common Cluster B disorder, marked by mood swings, impulsiveness, anger, and a fear of abandonment. Sometimes people with BPD find themselves going to extreme measures to avoid being forgotten or rejected. They have a hard time in relationships. This can extend to professional relationships as well as friendships and romantic attachments.

Cluster B disorders often go undiagnosed because they're so easy to dismiss. "Oh, she's just moody and high-strung." Popular culture gives us all kinds of excuses to look the other way. It's because she's Italian, she's a Virgo, she's an only child, the list goes on. Personal histories can allow us to write off this kind of symptom too. "It's because her last boyfriend was so arrogant," or "it's because her brother used to ignore her." But Tessa wasn't making excuses. She recognized her symptoms and wanted to deal with them head-on. I appreciated her bravery.

After getting to know Tessa a little more, I had the opportunity to meet her mother, Michelle. It was easy to recognize that Michelle had the same symptoms as Tessa, though Michelle had never been diagnosed with BPD. Tessa had done some searching in the family history and learned that doctors believed Michelle's mother had the same disorder. Michelle had avoided diagnosis—whether from fear or detachment, we can't be sure—but we thought perhaps now Tessa was paying the price of her mother's lack of healing.

There is no such thing as the perfect parent. All parents at one point or another will inadvertently cause a confusing or traumatic experience in their children's lives. It's one of the more difficult elements of our humanity. It's why we all need to heal and why healing is very often a lifelong process. But to truly heal, one must be willing to do the difficult work of removing the layers, of recognizing their own childhood trauma and drama, of learning lessons from them, and ultimately releasing them.

No healing journey is easy. In difficult times, it's essential to remind yourself that better days are coming. You won't always wake up in the morning with a heavy heart, I promise. You've survived a lot of the hard stuff already. Some of the storms you weathered, it's possible they didn't come to make life harder; possibly they came to clear a path. You're already en route to your better, brighter future, even if you don't feel it just yet.

For the days during your healing journey when your pain returns, remind yourself that the pain is only visiting, that it is temporary, and not moving in to stay. Your healing has arrived to stay—your healing is your new reality.

Remember too, you have the power to strengthen or modify your healing story at any moment, *you* get to choose. *You* are in the driver seat this time, you are no longer a victim of your childhood, where you didn't have the voice to speak up for yourself. In the words of Alexandra Elle *(How We Heal)*, we are not healing by mistake; we are healing with purpose.

You're not only healing to survive pain; you're healing to welcome in joy.

I want to say that I am sorry for the things in the past that hurt you. I believe you. I believe in you. You are not what happened to you. You are what you choose to become.

On the longer days of your healing journey, those days when the pain returns and fills you with fear, pain and insecurity, know that the pain is only visiting. You do not have to be afraid because that pain is not here to stay. Change takes time. Be kind to yourself.

You are showing yourself how much you love this life by learning to regulate your own nervous system and striving to understand your own trauma responses. This is brave, beautiful work. Let healing become your new reality.

THE HEALING EXERCISE

This guided meditation will gently explore your current emotions and use them as a doorway to access and heal past wounds. It is a VERY powerful process that can be used when you are feeling triggered and have strong emotions. It can also be used when you are not triggered, and have space and time for self-healing. This is a process of self-compassion and acceptance, and it is perfectly okay to move at your own pace. Trust that your body, mind, and spirit are guiding you towards healing.

Guided Healing Meditation—Using Present Emotions to Heal Past Trauma

Find a quiet and comfortable space where you won't be disturbed. Sit in a relaxed position. Close your eyes and take a deep breath in through your nose, and then slowly exhale through your mouth.

Allow your body to settle, feeling your feet connected to the ground, your hands resting gently in your lap or by your sides.

With each breath, imagine that you are becoming more grounded, more centered in your body. Let go of any tension you may be carrying, and with each exhale, release any stress or discomfort to the best of your ability.

You are safe here, and it's okay to be present with whatever emotions arise.

Now, gently bring your awareness to how you're feeling in this moment. What emotions are present for you right now? Don't judge them, simply notice. Are you feeling sadness, anger, fear, joy, frustration, or perhaps numbness?

If you're unsure, take a few moments to scan your body and notice where you may feel any tension, heaviness, tingling, or tightness. These physical sensations can give you clues about the emotions you are experiencing.

Give yourself permission to fully experience whatever emotions are present. They are a part of your experience right now, and they are valid.

Now, choose the emotion that feels most intense to you. Take a moment to honor this emotion. Give it a name, acknowledge it, let it be. You don't need to push it away, change it, or suppress it.

Say quietly to yourself, "I see you, I feel you, and I honor you."

As you connect with this emotion, ask yourself: "What part of me is experiencing this emotion?"

Observe that part of you with compassion and get a sense for it, noticing as many details as possible.

Allowing your curiosity to be your guide, without judgment or expectation, ask that part of you: "What do you want me to know?"

Allow your curiosity to be your guide, without judgment or expectation.

Now, ask yourself: "Is this emotion coming from a protective part of me, or is it a vulnerable part of me, at the core of my pain?" If you sense anger, defensiveness, numbness, or avoidance, know that this is most likely a protective part of you. It arises to shield you from deeper pain. Acknowledge its presence with gratitude. Silently say to it, "Thank you for trying to protect me. I see you, and I honor your role."

Now, without judgment, move toward the deeper, more tender emotion that this protector has been shielding you from. Trust whatever arises—whether it is sadness, fear, shame, or loneliness. You are beginning to access the core wound that needs healing. Gently ask this protector, "What are you trying to protect me from feeling?

Imagine this vulnerable part as a younger version of yourself, or as a presence within you that holds pain. You may see an image, recall a memory, simply feel its emotions, or get a sense of what this part is experiencing.

Let it know that you are here now, as the loving and compassionate version of yourself. Let it feel your presence, your warmth, and your care.

As you connect to this more vulnerable part, allow any thoughts, feelings, or sensations to emerge naturally. There is no need to force anything—just stay open and curious. Gently ask this part: "What do you want me to know?"

Now, take a moment to express gratitude to this part of you for showing up. It has been carrying pain for a long time, waiting to be seen and understood.

Imagine extending warmth and kindness to this part of you. Wrap it in a soft, glowing light. Speak to it gently: "I see you. I hear you."

"It's okay to feel this way. I am here for you now."

"You are safe. You are loved. You are enough."

Ask this part, "What do you need from me right now?" Maybe it needs comfort, validation, or simply to be acknowledged. Listen with an open heart. If words don't come, trust the emotions and sensations that arise.

Take a deep breath in, and as you exhale, invite this part of you to release any fear, pain, or sadness it has been holding onto.

If it is ready, imagine placing this burden into a stream, watching it gently flow away. Or see it being absorbed into the earth, where it can be transformed into healing energy. Trust this part of you to let go in the way that feels right.

If this part of you is not ready to let go, it's okay. Let it know that you will continue to be here, whenever it feels safe to release.

Now, imagine gently embracing this part of you, welcoming it back into your whole self. See it filling with light, love, and warmth. Feel a deep sense of unity as it merges back into your being, no longer separate or alone.

Take a few deep breaths, noticing any shifts in your body. Do you feel lighter? More at peace? Simply notice, without expectations. Acknowledge the healing that has taken place, and trust that this process will continue beyond this meditation.

When you are ready, gently bring your awareness back to the present moment. Wiggle your fingers and toes, grounding yourself in the here and now. Slowly open your eyes, carrying with you a sense of healing, connection, and self-compassion.

Know that this inner dialogue is always available to you. Whenever strong emotions arise, you can return to this process, deepening your relationship with all parts of yourself. You are whole, and you are worthy of love and healing.

THE ART OF CONFIDENCE

(see also: courage, assurance,
poise, determination)

onfidence is the feeling of trust that a person or thing is reliable. Self-confidence is trust and belief in oneself. Self-confidence involves a positive belief that one can generally accomplish what one wishes to do in the future. Self-confidence is not the same as self-esteem, which is an evaluation of one's worth.

It is believed that a child's internal monologue develops as early as twenty months old, becoming more active and developed as they reach ages five or six. There are many terms for this kind of intrapersonal communication, all referring to the simple phenomenon of talking to yourself in your head.

The conversations we have with ourselves are so important. They play an outsized role in our self-awareness and level of confidence throughout our lives. It's believed that the amount of internal monologue individuals engage in will vary greatly from person to person. Some of us have fairly quiet minds while other people have a gabfest going on in there. As far as researchers can tell, there seems to be no correlation between the amount of internal dialogue one has and their intelligence. In fact, many feel that intrapersonal communication is more closely related to intuition than intellect.

According to Lenny Shedletsky, a professor of communications at the University of Southern Maine, intrapersonal communication becomes most important when people have to make decisions. And adults tend to make decisions quickly "because they're operating on this intuitive basis of what they already believe." The foundations of our beliefs remain important—the things we take in as children.

I had been thinking of all of this when a healer shared with me that clients often tell her they hear their own inner voice as their childhood voice. I was amazed. She continued to say that we all get emotionally stuck at our childhood drama/trauma and that it takes deep work to heal and grow emotionally.

As an interesting aside: neuroscientists believe that most deaf people experience their inner voice visually. Dr. Giordon Stark, a researcher from Santa Cruz, confirms this in an article in *The Guardian*. Stark is deaf and communicates using ASL. His inner voice is a pair of hands signing words in his brain. The hands aren't usually connected to anything, he explains. If Stark needs to remind himself to buy milk, he signs the word milk in his mind. This feels natural for him, peaceful even. Isn't the human brain incredible?

No matter how our inner voice sounds (or looks), in best case scenarios, it is our first confidante and our oldest friend. But what if this friend sounds more like a cranky neighbor or Debbie Downer? Research from the National Science Foundation estimates that a person has 12,000 to 60,000 thoughts per day. The study also concludes that eighty percent of these will be negative. Eighty percent.

Obviously, this high volume can feed depression or anxiety very well. That's why so many forms of healing focus on limiting the negative self-talk that enters the mind and embracing positivity. Welcoming and keeping close our positive thoughts, opinions, and ideas is work we all have to do daily, no matter what challenges we face, no matter how old we are, or what part of our healing journey we find ourselves traveling.

Recently, the United Nations website updated its definition of the word "confidence." With so many teens and young adults at risk worldwide, terms like self-esteem, self-value, and confidence are part of a global discussion. Advocates arrived at this description: confidence is "having a realistic, inner sense of our capabilities." The UN website designates confidence as a "super skill" and goes on to say that "trusting ourselves and our abilities is crucial to managing emotional challenges and succeeding with goals in life. A healthy amount of confidence is essential to mental health and success and improves decision-making and resilience. The key to confidence is self-awareness, to allow ourselves to experience and reflect on even the most unpleasant emotions."

A parent's level of self-confidence has a direct impact on their parenting style as well as their relationship with others. As we discussed in Chapter Four: The Art of Intuition, having a strong sense of intuition will help increase one's confidence. To know that we are not alone, that we are divinely guided, increases our sense of self and our choices. When we can quiet our minds and get answers from within, our confidence will increase. This will help us make better decisions about ourselves and for our children.

Several years ago, Kenny and I were sitting at the breakfast table and Jordan had just joined us in the kitchen. He seemed extremely irritable and I knew within minutes that I needed to schedule an appointment with Jordan's psychiatrist to address his irritability and possibly (hopefully) increase his Zoloft. I was confident that his behavior and his level of happiness might shift if/when the psychiatrist increased his dosage. Kenny on the other hand thought I should stop worrying and said "he is fine!" But my gut, also known as a mother's intuition, told me otherwise.

The following day, I scheduled Jordan's appointment and my gut was right. Dr. D increased Jordan's dosage and within 24 hours, Kenny and I saw an improvement in Jordan's behavior and attitude. (I didn't need to tell Kenny "see, I was right," as that would have been my ego speaking. But I allowed this situation to increase my level of confidence.)

In traditional cognitive behavioral therapy, or CBT, there's careful discussion of boundaries, whether your healing journey includes building them high or taking some down. And it's true that our boundaries may change as we're healing. You're reconnecting with your true self and the once natural instincts that may have become dulled over time. For so many of us, this is tied to confidence.

You will become better at knowing what is right for you. It's gradual but it's a less complicated process than we might think. It's simply that the right things don't drain you— instead they fill you up with a sense of knowing, with the positivity you have been craving (even if you didn't always know the craving was there)!

Let's talk for a moment about feeling nervous. When I was young, before going on stage in the school play or giving an oral book report in class, my friends would say "Don't be nervous." I understood this to mean "Don't be scared." But nervousness encompasses more than fear and it's not something we can just shut off when we're told "stop feeling this way," or "don't feel like this."

Feeling nervous is to feel agitated or alarmed, to be anxious, or high strung. Ah, there we go. I wasn't scared as much as I was high strung.

When my oldest child William was little and I read stories to him, I would slow down so that we could really enjoy his book together. I was a working mom with a long to-do list, so when I say I would slow down, I don't mean to imply this was an easy thing for me to do. Slowing down often took an incredible effort for me.

One day we were in the library and I heard a librarian tell a parent "see it as you read it." The librarian went on to explain how seeing-in-the-mind is important, that if we are not seeing the story unfold in our mind's eye, our kids are not seeing it either. Slowing down allows our children to visualize—it allows us to see things clearly too. "Really, really see it," the librarian said.

What if we could slow down in other parts of our lives? What if we could give ourselves that grace? Michell C. Clark, author of *Eyes on the Road*, says things are scary "because they're unfamiliar, not because you're incapable. Being nervous is part of the process." We need to be mindful of effective ways to reduce the stress entering our bodies. Michell says "Lately I've been meditating and walking on the treadmill to help alleviate my stress."

Brianna Wiest (author of *The Mountain Is You*) reminds us to "turn off our spotlight complexes." We forget that acquaintances tend to take us at face value. "Nobody is thinking about you the way that you are thinking about you. Nobody is evaluating you that way." When we put aside our spotlight complex, anxiety dissipates, and we're better able to relax.

Here are some affirmations I like:

"I will be kind, compassionate, and loving with myself today and every day."

"I am worthy of my own approval. I love and accept myself and will continue to celebrate my growth. I embrace all that I am."

"I see the good in my life and know that I have a lot to be grateful for."

"I declare today that I am open and ready for good news tomorrow."

"I am spiritually secure and grateful for my accomplishments."

"When new opportunities come my way, I will welcome them properly."

"I am going to be the adult I needed when I was a child."

"I am going to be happy, loved, and living in my purpose."

Confidence isn't a "maybe she's born with it" kind of thing. It's a continuing education for most of us, one that may become an important point of reassurance. Often, we are too hard on ourselves while showing constant kindness to others. So, the long trek to finally reach our own individual self-confidence is priceless.

I've found that confidence comes also in the form of finding mindful friends and professionals to remain essential in your support system. There is nothing wrong with seeking (or needing) an all-star team of big hearts in your world.

Remember how the pain we felt when first trying to understand our children's challenges or our own was so informative? Sometimes that pain lingers in us, resurfaces. As I was working on this chapter I took a short break to attend Columbia University's Global Mental Health Event in New York. I was excited to be back in the city, mostly because I had planned to take a car out to New Jersey to visit Jordan at graduate school before returning to California.

While in Jersey, Jordan and I tried to get into his favorite Japanese restaurant but the wait was long and we were both hungry. We found another restaurant, a cool little tavern, and ended up having delicious meals. I told myself not to talk too much or ask too many questions because I didn't want to distance him. Being with Jordan could be a little like walking on eggshells sometimes. I needed to respect his needs and not push for too much information, knowing that could put him into a cranky mood.

We sat down at a table for two, decided what we were going to eat and then bam! He sprung it on me, the amazing news that he was accepted to the PhD program in mathematics! I couldn't help but cry, though I know that Jordan doesn't like for me to show big emotions in front of him. I couldn't help it and thankfully it didn't upset him. He said that he had already told Kenny and his siblings the day before. They had been in on his plan to share the news with me in person. I loved this. I was so happy for Jordan. And the timing of me being in New Jersey the day after he received his acceptance—it was a true gift from the Universe. Jordan then shared with me that he wasn't sure if he was going to accept that offer, he wasn't convinced that obtaining a Ph.D. was going to help him get further in life. I bit my tongue, held back my opinion, and prayed that he would accept the offer.

Dinner was going really well and we decided to share the s'mores desert our waiter had raved about. Then, out of nowhere, I saw Jordan's mannerisms beginning to change. I knew he was ready to go. He said that he didn't want to have dessert after all; he needed to return home to his work. I admit that I felt a little sad the evening was ending so quickly, but what was I to do?

We walked back to his apartment building. He showed me where the machine was to pay for the parking lot. We were about to say good-bye when I thought about how amazing his news was, how good it was to spend time with him, and asked him for a hug. He had his hands in his jacket and leaned in so I could hug him. He didn't pull his hands out of his pockets to hug back.

I walked away feeling broken. When I got into the car, I began to cry. I texted my good friend, who was a gifted psychic/medium, and told her what had just happened and how I was devastated. She responded immediately saying, "He will accept the PhD offer. Just don't push." Then a minute later she texted again. "Remember he is overwhelmed with emotion. He is filled up right now with something new, so he can't handle hugs."

Let me tell you, her message saved the day.

I felt hurt but it had not been his intention to hurt me. On top of that, I understood how his emotions were overwhelming to him. Isn't it amazing how our children's actions have such a profound effect on us, even though they do not intend them to? I've known for years that as parents we need to be both present and patient; that the members of my family do not emote at the same pace. I need to meet my now-adult children where they are.

In that moment, when Jordan was not going to hug back, I reverted to my earlier self, who just wanted her boy to jump into his mom's embrace and put his arms around her, like I imagined other boys did with their moms. After all these years I still had to check myself when the old thoughts crept into my brain: I just want us to be normal.

There is no such thing of course. Normal is just a construct. These are the things I work to help others accept. Still, I had to remind myself. Jordan and I had enjoyed a lovely dinner and shared amazing news. When my tears came, my friend had been there, a text away, to help me re-center, to give me those priceless, intuitive reminders.

Let's accept help when we need it—even when we don't. Our vast emotional landscapes hold valuable hints to guide our healing. The Universe teaches me again and again that we are spiritual people having human experiences. Our children, in their own ways, are having their own experiences, and we need to observe from the sidelines. As parents, we are not here simply to guide them. We learn from them too, from the vibrant moments we observe with them. We are here to be humbled. We gain confidence—in learning and relearning, in friendship, in experiences—to ensure our forward momentum, and that is an extraordinary thing.

There is discussion across disciplines about awakening our imaginations. When something goes awry in a scientific experiment, within a political issue, etc., we so often call it a "lack of data" or "lack of intelligence," when it's more accurately "a lack of imagination." But what is imagination exactly?

This is a profound question and one that I will answer according to my own experiences and those of some of my clients. This is where science meets spirituality and not everyone will agree on my interpretation. However, didn't many people walking the Earth believe the world was flat until we learned that it was round? Please read the following with an open mind.

When I was having my manic episode in May 2014, I knew what I was going through seemed batshit cray-cray to others. But to me, my mind had never been clearer. If it wasn't for my therapist, Rabbi, and oldest son, I would have thought that I was crazy. As I've said before, if this happened to me twenty years ago, they would have locked me up and thrown away the key. Luckily this wasn't my destiny. It breaks my heart to read about gifted people who went through a spiritual experience like mine and were subsequently locked up, or medicated beyond recognition, and that was the end of their creative and promising life as they had known it.

Being in a manic episode sounds to many like the equivalent of tripping on drugs (which I have never done so I cannot be sure) but this is a precarious comparison. The difference is that people who actually search out this experience, who take ayahuasca, for example, or other types of plant medicines that create "a trip"—they are actively seeking out a spiritual experience. They take on this altered state with curiosity or within a need for experimentation. For me, I was literally in over my head within this experience, with no intention, no training, and no one to guide me.

I will never forget that morning in May when I woke up around 5:00 a.m., I tapped on my husband's back and asked him if he was awake. He responded by saying "I have been waiting for your knock" which shocked me but also made sense in a weird way. I went outside to the balcony, followed by one of our doggies, and proceeded to lie on the lounge chair. I remember breathing in the air which seemed different than usual. It seemed heavenly, as if I was breathing in a whip-it—I had done one in high school—and I remember saying out loud "God, is that you?" One of my dogs was sitting on my lap and her head was facing the sky. I knew that she felt it too.

I ended up going back to sleep and woke up after everyone had left the house. I walked down stairs and felt a little dazed. It was then that I heard a loud voice say, "I saved your soul, now you will do what I say." I knew that my soul had been saved because I had gone from a place of not believing in God or the Universe to feeling like I was one with God. If I wasn't in a heightened state, I truly believe that I would have dropped dead from a heart attack. I was both shocked and frightened. I was too scared to speak, but I thought to myself, God is that you? I felt that yes, my soul had been saved. I had gone from a place of darkness to pure light and love but couldn't quite grasp what more was happening.

Later that day, I was taking care of my friend's ten-year-old son, Adam, and we were watching TV. I felt as if the television was speaking to me. Impulsively I began taking notes. I quickly grew concerned and called my therapist. He was able to squeeze me in that same afternoon.

I arrived at Dr. H's office with Adam and it was as if Dr. H was expecting Adam to be with me. He immediately took Adam to play in the back of the room and came back to sit with me. This is when I needed to decide if I was going to be totally honest with Dr. H.—I had some fear of him sending me away to a mental institution—but I needed to share my experience with someone.

I told Dr. H what had occurred, both in the bedroom and in the kitchen; that I heard a voice speak out loud to me. I held my breath waiting for his response. This was the telling moment. I was terrified by the possibilities and trying to predict what was about to come out of his mouth. Thankfully, Dr. H responded by asking me if I thought that it was Divine Intervention. I finally exhaled and responded, Absolutely!

I then asked him when he became spiritual. He said about eight years ago. He went through something similar, and felt that maybe he went through that so he could be equipped to work with me now. I was amazed and relieved.

He advised me to see a pychiatrist; he could tell that I was manic and needed to be brought back down to planet earth. It was this experience that has been one of the greatest attributes to building my confidence. Knowing that I was not alone and that there is a Higher Power that is constantly guiding me—this assurance from my therapist was so powerful.

However, once I was medicated and came "back to planet earth," my connection with my spirituality diminished and my confidence was once again challenged. It has taken years and years of healing to help build my confidence and to be able to publish this book. I felt that my story was too "woo-woo" to share, but I have come to terms with knowing that my truth is the truth; it is my experience and it doesn't matter what others think about me or my story.

One way to help us build our confidence is to journal. It's amazing what we end up writing about once we let the pen hit the paper. If you have never journaled, why not try experimenting with it now? There are no rules or instructions—your journal can be anything you want it to be. Studies conducted during the past forty years in both clinical and educational settings have found that journaling boosts feelings of well-being, reduces anxiety and stress, improves clarity, and supports self-love and acceptance.

A friend who journals frequently told me that she can read past journal entries and literally see her confidence growing from one month to the next. A 2017 study in the Journal of Biobehavioral Medicine showed that adults and teenagers who journaled through their challenges achieved physical benefits as well. There was a sharp decrease in blood pressure for those with hypertension, as well as increased immune system function for most participants who journaled three to five times a week for fifteen to twenty-minute sessions. Future moments where you look back at your journals might be amazing.

These days in popular culture we are reminded to love ourselves.

I consider this progress!

When your confidence is low, give yourself a pep talk. Speak to yourself the same way that you would speak to a child. We are often harder on ourselves than we are on others. "Look at you, doing the work, getting out there, making it happen. You're doing a great job pushing through anxieties, facing your fears, learning from your mistakes. You know it's not easy and it's not fun, not always anyway, but you're making progress, you're doing the things, you're on the path to your own brighter future." Honor your energy. Trust your instincts. Hear what your body tells you. Love and celebrate your mind in the same way that you want your children to celebrate and love theirs.

Fall in love with the journey of becoming the very best version of yourself. Step into joy and peace. At times you will feel your forward momentum is leading you; other times you will feel it's guiding you. Both things are true. Do not lose sight of how far you've traveled.

Make friends with others committed to personal growth. It's when we start to really work together and connect that the profound growth happens. Billy Chapata, author of *Flowers on the Moon*, puts it like this. "You heal every time you break out of a cycle of letting hurt versions of your inner child make decisions for you as an adult."

You will know you're healing when you no longer feel the need to seek approval from others; when you no longer need that kind of acceptance. This is because you are affirming yourself on a regular basis. You no longer need their praise to make you feel whole.

You are the greatest project you'll ever work on. And to make way in the project, you'll have moments when you need to reset, restart, refocus. Do that as many times as you need to. Just promise me you will never give up on such an excellent work in progress. Stay close to the people who want more for you—not more from you.

A thing we do need is laughter—apologies if I sound like a broken record on this point. For my foundation's annual fundraiser, we plan a comedy night because laughing is powerful. Before I became a parent, I had no idea how much laughing with my kids would heal my heart. Those little humans had no idea how much light they brought to my life, and this is still true now that they are adults. Laughing with family and friends and even with strangers is a true gift. There are no perfect parents, no perfect children, or marriages, or friendships, but there are so many perfect moments along the way. And when it comes to speaking about challenges with our children, we need to laugh often in addition to a good cry once in a while.

A friend suggested this to me recently: go laugh in a place where you used to cry. "Change the energy," they said, "let confidence grow from softness."

Bianca Sparacino, the author of *The Strength in Our Scars*, reminds us to stop trying to make ourselves indestructible. "Like any soft creature it is in your nature to break; like any soft creature it is in your nature to heal."

THE CONFIDENCE EXERCISES

Confidence is not about becoming someone new. It is about uncovering the wholeness that already exists within you. At times, the way we speak to ourselves can be our greatest obstacle. The critical inner voice, shaped by past experiences, can diminish our self-worth and create patterns of self-doubt. But just as this voice was learned, it can also be unlearned.

This exercise will guide you through a process that transforms your inner dialogue, helping you build self-confidence from the inside out. Through awareness, self-compassion, and intentional shifts in thought patterns, you will reconnect with the strength and worthiness that have always been within you.

This practice is not about silencing or rejecting your inner critic. Instead, you will meet it with love and understanding and shift your inner dialogue to a more compassionate voice. As you go through this process, trust that every step forward—no matter how small—is a powerful act of reclaiming your confidence and self-trust. You got this!

Exercise One: Journal Activity - Transforming Your Inner Dialogue and Building Self-Confidence

What role does your inner dialogue play in you life? How can self-care journaling support us in building confidence? Please visit marajjames.com for more journal exercises and insights.

Step One: Recognize the critical inner voice.

The first step in building confidence is awareness. Many people aren't fully conscious of how harsh their inner dialogue is. They may have internalized critical messages over the years, often from external sources, but they don't realize how much it impacts their self-esteem and confidence.

- Over the next few days, observe your inner dialogue without judgment. Note when you are critical or harsh towards yourself. Write down any recurring thoughts, such as "I'm not good enough," "I always mess things up," "I can't do this," or "I should have done better." Notice how this inner voice is a thought that is part of your experience, but it is NOT who you are.

Step Two: Rewrite your negative beliefs.

Now it's time to challenge the truth of your inner critic. This involves questioning the validity of those negative thoughts and replacing them with empowering, compassionate ones.

- Question the inner critic - For each critical recurring thought, ask yourself:

  o Is this thought based on the truth of who I am, or assumptions I have about me?

  o Would I say this to a young child, a good friend, or a loved one?

  o What evidence do I have that contradicts this thought?

- Replace your inner critic thoughts with compassionate ones: For each critical thought, create a more supportive and loving one. Imagine speaking to a loved young child. What would you say to them?

  For example, if you think, "I am so stupid," replace it with, "I made a mistake, and I can learn and grow from it."

  Write down your supportive responses to each critical thought as you cultivate a more positive inner voice.

- Affirmations of Self-Confidence: Develop a list of positive affirmations that resonate with you. Say them daily, especially when you feel your inner critic trying to take over.

Examples:

- o *"I am worthy of love and respect."*

- o *"I am capable of growing and learning."*

- o *"I am doing the best I can, and that is enough."*

- o *"I choose to let go of self-judgment."*

- o *"I am deserving of kindness, love, and understanding."*

- o *"I am that I am, and that is enough."*

Step Three: Develop positive self-talk.

Just like any new habit, the more you practice positive self-talk, the easier it becomes to shift from a critical inner dialogue to one that fosters peace, confidence, and capability. Developing this new way of thinking requires daily awareness and conscious redirection of your thoughts.

Start by setting aside time each day to affirm your self-worth with the positive statements you created in step two, adding new ones as needed. If an affirmation feels forced or untrue, adjust it to something you genuinely believe. The key is to create statements that support and uplift you.

As you move through your day, become mindful of moments when your inner critic surfaces. When you catch yourself engaging in negative self-talk, pause. Instead of allowing the critical voice to take over, gently redirect your thoughts to a more supportive and compassionate perspective.

Remember, healing and growth are ongoing journeys. Be gentle with yourself, and celebrate each step forward, no matter how small.

Exercise Two: Releasing Guilt and Shame

When it comes to parenting, guilt and shame are common emotions. They can be overwhelming, especially for mothers. These emotions can disconnect you from yourself, creating self-doubt and diminishing your confidence. Releasing them is a deeply transformative process, empowering you to build your confidence and a stronger connection to your inner knowing. The journey to confidence includes shifting guilt and shame, and gradually embracing yourself as a parent that is learning and growing. This is not about achieving perfection as a parent, but about embracing your vulnerabilities with acceptance and self-love.

This guided meditation is designed to help you release guilt and shame around parenting, and build a stronger and more loving connection to your child.

The Releasing Guilt and Shame Meditation

Find a quiet space, close your eyes, and take a deep, grounding breath in… Slowly exhale. With each breath, allow your body to soften, releasing any tension. Let each breath deepen your connection with yourself.

Now, bring to mind any feelings of guilt or shame you may have as a parent. Notice where it lives in your body—perhaps a heaviness in your chest or a tightness in your stomach. Instead of resisting, simply acknowledge it. Breathe into it.

Guilt and shame tend to weigh you down— keeping you disconnected from yourself, your child, and the love that is always present. These emotions do not make you a better parent; they only drain your energy and keep you trapped in self-doubt. You cannot grow from a place of shame. You cannot show up fully for your child when you are disconnected from your own heart.

Take a deep breath in... and as you exhale, envision the guilt and shame leaving your body with your breath, letting go of these heavy emotions that no longer serve you. Notice the burden of guilt and shame gently lifting away. You are not meant to hold onto this.

Take a few more breaths, breathing into any lingering guilt, shame, or heaviness, and exhaling out those sensations fully, until you feel a sense of release.

Now, place your hand over your heart and feel the truth of these words: "I am doing the best I can with what I know at this time. I am learning. I am growing. I am enough." Let these words sink in, dissolving any lingering self-judgment.

Visualize a warm, golden light glowing in your heart—this is the energy of self-love and wisdom. With every breath, feel it expand, filling your heart with understanding, self-compassion, and deep trust in yourself.

Every challenge you face as a parent is here to teach you something—not to punish you, but to help you grow. Your child is here to help guide you deeper into love, patience, and presence. Parenting is not about perfection; it is about connection. And that connection begins with you.

See yourself now—not through the old lens of guilt and shame, but through the lens of truth: a parent who is learning, growing, and doing their best with an open heart. Your love is enough. You are enough, just as you are.

Take a deep breath in… and as you exhale, step fully into confidence, knowing that you are growing in every moment. Trust yourself. Trust the journey.

When you feel ready, gently open your eyes, carrying this renewed sense of self-acceptance and confidence with you.

9

THE ART OF GRATITUDE

(see also: recognition, honor, grace)

*W*hen I receive letters like this one, I cannot help but feel incredibly grateful that I am here doing this work, connecting with others on their healing journeys.

" … within the first five minutes I knew I had found exactly the support we needed … I realized that my own healing is the key to helping my son. I feel empowered and I finally see a path forward for our family."

The simple explanation of gratitude is "the quality of being thankful; readiness to show appreciation for and to return kindness." In the Bible, gratitude is mentioned many times and it is said to help people develop the fruits of the Spirit.

Research suggests that gratitude can have many, many benefits for both physical and mental health. Grateful people are more likely to stay hopeful and maintain a positive outlook when faced with adversity or stress. In regards to mental health, gratitude can reduce harmful emotions including anger, envy, frustration, and resentment. Gratitude can also increase positive emotions, which can lead to more happiness and less depression.

Having made expressions of gratitude during the day can also help people sleep better and longer by calming the nervous system and combating anxious thoughts. Oprah Winfrey ends each day by listing five things she is grateful for—those can be small details, or big events, but either way she has ended the day with gratitude. This may be my favorite of "Oprah's favorite things." If it works for Oprah it just might work for the rest of us.

My dear friend and healer, Renata, (whose talents are beautifully reflected in this book) has spent her career studying mind-body connections. Helping people sleep better is a major point of her healing work. She looks at mind-body intelligence with an eye toward creating balance, whereas in western medicine professionals might look at mind-body intelligence as a path to diagnosis. She asks her clients "How are you sleeping?" even if they did not come to her with a sleep issue. She looks for connections and root causes for various issues.

We share the human experience collectively, Renata points out, but we have unique-ness, originality. I think some of that originality occurs in the way we experience and express gratitude. The problem is that in our busy lives, too many of us skip over moments of gratitude. We neglect expressing how grateful we are for the good in our lives, especially on days when things go badly.

As a guest on my podcast, Renata explained that she loves the word "entity." It's a beautiful word. "Whether an entity is a company, an organization, a club, a book, it is also an energy form. You can look at an entity and observe 'How is this energy form operating?' What is shifting? What energy work can we do?" She suggests that we approach complica-tions as opportunities for healing. At the end of the day we want our own experience to make a difference, we want to show gratitude, we want to help others. "The more we can trust in the Universe," Renata says, "the more we can accept its clues."

The actor and wellness advocate Kelly Rutherford posted something so beautiful on social media. She wrote "The whole world is a series of miracles, but we're so used to them we call them ordinary things."

With gratitude as a practice, we can experience more joy and peace in our lives. Who couldn't use more of this? Something we do not discuss enough is the relationship between joy and peace. Can my individual happiness really help to make the world a more peace-ful place? It's mind-blowing but the answer is YES! Let's talk about what joy is exactly. It is more than a quiet happiness. Joy is the opposite of violence. Joy is a wonderful force in the world. It is love at the moment when love is blazing into action. It is a natural product of the natural world. If only we had more of it.

Does everything happen for a reason? I wish I knew definitively the answer. It's hard for many people in the Western world, when we suffer a trauma, to negotiate in our mind that this pain is ours for a reason, that today may be difficult, but the path leads some-where we need to go. And that there is a light at the end of each tunnel. Two decades ago there was a bombing in Kuta, a tourist enclave in Bali, Indonesia. While the Western media covered around the clock the terrorist activity that had preceded the attack, Balinese resi-dents refused to speculate when approached by reporters. Most said something like "God must be upset with the way we are living to have allowed such a cruel thing to happen here." One said simply, "We must all take a closer look at our lives." It was remarkable to many Western viewers that within this horrific tragedy residents did not show anger or resentment; they showed introspection and concern.

Locals expressed their condolences, and had remarkable public ceremonies for the deceased and injured. They felt the tragedy fully, but you could sense their words carried gratitude as well as deep sorrow. No matter how horribly it had come to them, they found value in the message: *we must all take a closer look at our lives.*

As I mentioned earlier, it is so important for us to put our own oxygen masks on first so that we have full, happy hearts and minds with which to best serve others. This includes our children and spouses in their down moments, without letting them push our buttons or affect our moods. This is where self-care comes into play.

Let's never confuse self-care with selfishness. Being a parent or a spouse by nature can minimize one's self-absorption, but we must not let the pendulum swing too far in the other direction. We want to never disappear. When our children or spouse (or anyone else) needs more from us, we must be reminded to stay connected to ourselves and our environments as well as to them and not lose ourselves in the process. Self-care is not simply a buzz word; self-care is wisdom and survival.

We have often heard that laughing and crying have a lot in common. Sometimes we need our crying as a form of release. Sometimes we go with laughter simply because it feels better. I once took an outdoor yoga class where we were asked to lie down on our mats. I waited for instruction to move into a pose, hoping it would not be too difficult, ha. Instead the teacher invited us to start laughing, to just lie there in laughter. It was wonderful, feeling our faces relax, hearing chuckles and giggles around us become hilarious, just to lie there laughing as clouds moved above in a beautiful bright blue sky.

I hope you'll try it sometime. Lie down outside, look to the sky, think of something funny and laugh. I think it's even more inspiring than a warrior pose. But you'll need the warrior stuff too!

I'm grateful for the strength other people inspire in me, even in the circumstances where I am heartbroken by the traumas that have informed or challenged their strength. In May 2014, during my manic episode/spiritual awakening, William, my oldest son, was in his Freshman year at UC Santa Barbara when the Isla Vista shooting occurred. The perpetrator, a 22-year-old college student, murdered six people, injured fourteen, then took his own life. Ten years later it's still difficult to talk about, to even write these words.

The killing spree started with the stabbing of his roommates and one of their friends. The killer emailed his parents, his therapist, and a friend a manuscript of more than one hundred pages where he expressed his inability to find a girlfriend, his hatred for women, and how he despised happy couples. He wrote of resentment toward his classmates, his parents, and dissatisfaction with his family and his childhood. After sending the email, he uploaded an angry video to YouTube, where he spoke of "retribution."

The therapist immediately alerted his mother to the email. His parents quickly called campus security and the police, then they raced from their homes in Los Angeles to Isla Vista, but they were too late to stop or even understand what their son had started.

It was too horrific to comprehend, this terror unleashed in an idyllic little town where my son was only just starting his college career. Kenny and I were beside ourselves, relieved that William was alive, at the same time heartbroken for the families of those who were not.

The story was covered by the media around the world as an act of misogynistic terror. It was impossible to watch television, the talking heads discussing the true horrors of the young man's instability and anger, mental health experts cringing as their own introductions were read from teleprompters—no one wants to be an expert within this context, ever.

The pain being felt on campus and beyond—it was impossible to describe then and I'm still at a loss years later. It was hard to know what to say to William. You can't properly help your child make sense of something like this because it doesn't make sense. When I learned from William that one of the victims of the tragedy was a close friend, the horror became even more personal and heartbreaking for our family. None of us could find the right words.

The sadness was overwhelming, and I was already in a fragile state, but I knew that the Universe had a plan for me. I could not explain it well at the time, but I felt motivated, even under all this sadness and despair. I felt in many moments that week that God was signaling me—this was one of them. God was calling me to find the confidence and endurance to do something that could make a difference, but what?

The answer came to me several months later as I embarked upon my own healing journey. I knew that I needed to help those suffering from emotional and mental health challenges and I needed to share with others how holistic healing modalities can assist in a way that I never knew possible. I had an important realization. It was possible that my younger son, Jordan, could have carried rage and confusion his entire life, somewhat like the shooter, if he had not been properly supported with medication and therapy, in addition to some amazing holistic healers. I am forever grateful that he is now living a happy life and it breaks my heart to see others suffering.

It's not a comfortable thought but it's an important one. What if Jordan had not had our healers to help him remove the darkness he had experienced? What if the anger that filled him when he was younger—that seemed to come out of nowhere—had taken over?

What if the support and efforts of our family had been inadequate or misguided in some way? What if the anger had stayed there, building up within him? Jordan was lucky that he was able to be stabilized, but what about the children who hadn't been, who were still on some kind of ledge?

While Jordan was a very different young man than the shooter, I read how the shooter had grown up with a mother who loved him. She had wanted healthy outcomes for him but something crucial had been missing and a previously unimaginable horror became a deeply tragic reality.

Anger and anxiety take such a toll on a young mind; on any mind. I don't mean to over-simplify an obviously complex and intensely painful situation, but I had to wonder: how easily could our family, or any family, have suddenly found themselves on the other side of this horror story?

We are constantly reading terms like "anger management" and "mood regulation," but what can we actually do on a daily basis, within our communities, our families, and ourselves, to minimize anger and violence in the world and move toward peace and joy?

In the *Book of Joy,* the Archbishop Desmond Tutu and the Dalai Lama agree that a compassionate concern for the well-being of others is a great source of happiness. Joy is a destination on our family journeys. So is laughter. There is so much seriousness in the world. We need to hear ourselves and one another laughing more.

I don't remember the word empathy popping up a lot when I was growing up, but there was certain phrasing that suggested we take our own abilities in this area seriously, like "put yourself in her shoes." Several years ago, a book by Leslie Jamison called *The Empathy Exams* was making headlines. The book asked people to consider what does it mean exactly to feel someone else's pain?

Something that I found intriguing was Jamison's background: she had previously worked as a medical actor, paid to act out symptoms for medical students to diagnose. I loved this. The doctors in my family can easily recall these assignments. I know that many other caretakers, including teachers, have experienced similar exercises in their own professional development endeavors.

It occurred to me that we might try this in many professions, whether you're training to be a babysitter, an attorney, or a hotel concierge. An actor comes in and gives an empathetic portrayal of an unexpected event. Then we're asked, okay, what might be going on with this child/client/guest? Such an exercise engages our imaginations—the very best problem-solving tool we have. Let's think of it like this: there is room for empathy in every human endeavor.

Empathy is, to me, the highest form of human knowledge.

When we're talking about empathy, we're focusing on acknowledging circumstances, confronting pain, sharing grief or joy. We're talking really about human connection, that thing we all need, even if we need it in different doses. Empathy, three beautiful syllables, together pretty enough to be a little girl's name. If you grew up reading *Beezus and Ramona* books you might remember the story of Ramona's doll, whom she named Chevrolet. Beezus protested. That's the name of a car, Ramona, you cannot name your doll that. Yes I can, Ramona said. She explained, "It's a pretty word and now I'll get to say it all the time." I think this is a story where the reader is meant to identify with Beezus, but I have to say, I love Ramona! And this is sort of how I feel about the word *empathy*. It's a beautiful word. I want to live in a world where we say it—and experience it—all the time.

Gratitude is also linked to courage. Have the courage to give voice to exactly how grateful you feel. Be bold in creating space for you, in growing, in becoming the best version of yourself. Be brave enough to slow down, to really see the things that are good for you, to soak in warmth and nourishing moments. Practice the pause, as they say. Acknowledge where you are and how far you have come. Look after *you*. Allow yourself deeper levels of curiosity. Celebrate the little things, the details, the simple things in a world full of complexity.

I am forever grateful for my parenting journey because becoming a parent means learning strengths you didn't know you had. Parenthood is inspiring, draining, daring, gut-wrenching, beautiful and chaotic, all in the same day, or sometimes, even within the same hour. You learn a lot about your fears. It is a disorienting thing to acknowledge how much fear one human body can hold and how much emotional work we do to move beyond those fears.

A recent "Talk of the Town" piece in *The New Yorker* tells the story of a man named Jamie Livingston. When Jamie was a student at Bard College, he decided he would take one Polaroid™ photo each day. Only one—he was strict about that. His friend David recalled that he "had a kind of spidey sense for the right moment." Jamie stored the photos, which he faithfully dated, in a small suitcase.

David would later describe them as alternately beautiful, mysterious, and mundane. There are gargoyles and clarinets, crowds in restaurants, friends sunbathing, the West Side Highway. Jamie died young, on his forty-first birthday, with cancer. His friends compiled his photos into an exhibition that could be viewed in person or online. I'm not sure whether to call it a visual memoir or biography. Maybe it's a map or a time capsule.

Whatever we call it, I'm moved by the simple act that Jamie did faithfully each day without knowing that one day the collection would be interesting to viewers all over the world. And beautifully, those recorded moments became a comfort to his friends. It got me thinking about things that we might do every day, not as a necessity or an obligation or an assignment, but just to delight in noticing the world around us, in the beauty of a quiet ritual.

A colleague, Tricia, who lived in the city for most of her life, recently retired to the desert. She carries a little notebook in which she draws a new cactus each day. Who knew there were so many kinds? An acquaintance, Barbara, spent the summer caring for a friend on the Mendocino coast. She kept a small glass jar in her bedroom. Every afternoon when she walked on the beach, she collected a miniature piece of sea glass to add to the jar. By the end of August, the jar had the most wonderful and soothing kaleidoscope of colors.

What is something you might like to do every day? Is there room for a quiet ritual in your life?

It is amazing to me that in these quiet rituals we can reflect and show gratitude for the world around us. In the quiet rituals live our caring, our softness, our imaginations.

Gloria Steinem once said "without leaps of imagination or dreaming, we lose the excitement of possibilities. Dreaming, after all, is a form of planning."

Let's keep dreaming, planning and caring.

Children will multiply whatever you give them. If you give them anger or frustration, they will return that in abundance. So, imagine giving them expressions of your love, giving your attention, your time, imagine showing them curiosity and positivity. Those things will come back to you in incredible ways—and an amazing human will grow up before your very eyes.

Show them friendship. You're never too old to live by the lyrics of one of my favorite summer camp songs. "Make new friends, but keep the old. One is silver and the other gold." Having the support of a true and constant mom-friend is a blessing, the kind of person who is there for you even if your journey and choices as a parent are different from hers. Someone who's there for you whether or not they truly understand your challenges—that's also love.

We rise by lifting others; we're able to lift others when we release our personal trauma and connect in new ways to the world around us.

So let's be crazy-amazing!

Let's continue to grow, learn, heal and love.

THE GRATITUDE EXERCISES

Gratitude is a powerful practice that shifts your focus from what is lacking to what is abundant in your life. By intentionally cultivating gratitude, you begin to transform your inner experience fostering greater inner peace.

Attitude of Gratitude Meditation

Place one hand over your heart, and begin to tune in to the natural rhythm of your breath.

Begin to deepen your breath, inhaling slowly to the count of five… and exhaling gently to the count of five.

> Inhale slowly…
> 1… 2… 3… 4… 5…
>
> Exhale gently…
> 1… 2… 3… 4… 5…
>
> Inhale slowly…
> 1… 2… 3… 4… 5…
>
> Exhale gently…
> 1… 2… 3… 4… 5…

Continue this breathing rhythm until smooth and steady.

With each inhale, feel your breath nourishing your heart.

With each exhale, allow any tension or distractions to melt away.

This simple breath—combined with the energy of gratitude—begins to open your heart.

It gently awakens the heart-brain connection, creating a space of inner coherence, calm, and clarity.

Keeping your connection to this deeper and smoother breath, recall something or someone you deeply appreciate—this could be a person, an experience, a lesson learned, or even a small moment of joy. Allow yourself to fully feel the warmth of this gratitude, letting it expand in your chest.

Notice this sense of gratitude filling your whole body by connecting to more things in your life you are grateful for. Notice how your energy shifts as your gratitude expands.

Make this practice a daily ritual, allowing gratitude to become a natural state through which you experience life. By choosing gratitude in every situation, you cultivate resilience, inner peace, and a greater sense of connection to yourself and to the world around you. Trust that with consistent practice, gratitude will transform not only your perspective, but your entire way of being.

EPILOGUE

(see also: postscript, coda)

Go ahead and just love your crazy-charmed life. Keep showing your children and yourself the best of YOU! Try new healing modalities. Try new foods. Write weird things in your journal. Tell your people you love them. Do the things you didn't think you had time to do.

Experience the things you're no longer afraid of. Be generous and mindful. Start thinking bigger. Take your life and make it the best story you have ever written. Papa gave us this thing called life, and it's a beautiful gift.

A monarch butterfly has notably delicate wings but is equipped with two sets of them. Their adulthood lasts only a few weeks yet a single monarch can travel thousands of miles. Monarch migration is said to be the greatest phenomena in the natural world.

My favorite feeling in the world—my own personal phenomena—is laughing with William, Rachel, Jordan, and Kenny, and realizing mid-laugh not only how intensely I love them, but how much Kenny and I truly enjoy our kids' wisdom, humor and verve—how much we delight in their very existence. Our journeys, independently and collectively, have been a thousand different things, including unpredictable. And it will be my greatest honor to see this family grow. (As I write this, William is engaged! His fiancé is a bright and beautiful addition to our growing family!)

To my family, and all we have faced, I am endlessly grateful.

To Papa-God, thanks for showing up, even in those early days when I would have sworn I didn't need you. Indeed, you've shown me. I did and I do. We all do.

To my own inner child: I see you. I will never stop nurturing you and I am ALWAYS here for you!

To the person I was, I love you.

To the person I am, I'm proud of you.

To the person I'm becoming, I'm so excited for you.

To my amazing clients—both private clients and those who have connected through our HUGS Healing Center—it is one of the great honors of my life to work with you.

To those who have traveled these pages with me, thank you from the bottom of my heart. I'm cheering for you and your own personal healing journeys. You got this!

THE BONUS EXERCISE

I deeply appreciate your openness and participation in the exercises throughout this book. Your commitment to the journey of healing and growth is truly inspiring.

As we close this journey together, I want to express my deep gratitude to my incredible friend and healer, Renata, whose wisdom and support have guided these exercises.

A special gift to you, Renata and I are delighted to offer a yummy sound bowl healing experience, designed to help you integrate and embody the transformative work we've explored together. Please join us at marajjames.com.

Sealing Your Healing and Embracing Your Wholeness Sound Bowl Meditation

Find a quiet, comfortable space where you can relax. Gently close your eyes and take a deep breath in. Exhale slowly. Feel your body settle, your shoulders soften, and your heart open to this moment.

With each inhale, welcome in a sense of peace . . . and with each exhale, release any tension, any weight that you've been carrying. Allow yourself to arrive fully here, now.

Bring your awareness to your heart. Imagine a warm, golden light glowing softly in your chest, radiating warmth, safety, and love. This is your inner light, always present, always guiding you.

Feel this light expand with every breath, filling your entire body with a deep sense of love and acceptance. Know that you are held, you are seen, you are enough—exactly as you are.

Now, gently place your hands over your heart and silently whisper to yourself, "I am loved. I am supported. I am whole." Let these words sink into your being like a warm embrace.

If there are parts of you that feel wounded, scared, or uncertain, invite them into this space of love. Let them be cradled by the warmth of your heart. Let them know they belong.

Imagine the Universe, or a loving presence of your choosing, wrapping around you like a protective cocoon of light. You are never alone. You are always guided. You are deeply, unconditionally loved.

Breathe in this love . . . and as you exhale, feel any lingering doubts or fears melt away. Feel your heart open wider, ready to give and receive love freely.

Now, slowly bring your awareness back to the present moment. Take a deep, nourishing breath, wiggle your fingers and toes, and when you feel ready, gently open your eyes.

Know that you can return to this love, this strength, and this deep connection anytime. It is always within you. You are enough. You are loved. You are whole.

The journey continues . . .

Please join us online for the
Unconditional: Mental Health Redefined Book Club
including special activities and events.

marajjames.com

ACKNOWLEDGEMENTS

(see also: recognition, declaration, affirmation)

*T*hank you to my team for helping create this work of "art" (pun intended) including Stacy Bierlein, Keisha Clark, Lee Nagan, Anthony Piersanti, and Renata Ururahy. Without their efforts this would still be a draft hanging out in Google Docs™.

I am eternally thankful to my amazing family for always being there for me, especially through the rough times. My children have been my greatest gift as well as the greatest teachers of my life.

My husband Kenneth has and will always be my pillar of strength and support. As I always say, that which doesn't kill us makes us stronger. I am grateful that my husband and I together have grown stronger and more united and that the best is yet to come!

Thank you to my family's gifted physicians, therapists, and healers. Without your knowledge, wisdom, and healing abilities, I cannot even imagine where we would be today. I admire your work and will continue to sing your praises.

Special thanks to my readers and listeners. For those wishing to ask questions or seeking additional guidance on healing journeys, please reach out to me via my website marajjames.com. I look forward to hearing from you!

Mara J James is Founder and CEO of the Extraordinary Lives Foundation nonprofit organization and the HUGS Healing Center. Her *Piggie Bear*® children's book series is celebrated in learning centers nationwide. She and her husband, Dr. Kenneth James, first met as students at the University of Rochester and now have the honor to be parents to three amazing adult children. They live in Southern California.

www.ingramcontent.com/pod-product-compliance
Lightning Source LLC
Chambersburg PA
CBHW041537120626

46551CB00019B/2727